THE W
WILDLIFE RESERVE

THE WHITE GRASS PLAINS WILDLIFE RESERVE

THE SUKILA PHANTA : THE JEWEL IN THE CROWN

Peter Byrne

Published by
PILGRIMS PUBLISHING

Distributed by
PILGRIMS BOOK HOUSE
B 27/98 A-8, Nawabganj Road
Durga Kund, Varanasi-221010, India
Tel: 91-542-2314059
E-mail: pilgrims@satyam.net.in
Website: www.pilgrimsbooks.com

First Edition 2008
Copyright © 2008, Peter Byrne
All Rights Reserved

Layout & Cover design by Asha Mishra

ISBN 978-81-7769-663-2
[BDK 81-7769-663-2]

The contents of this book may not be reproduced, stored in any form—printed, electronic, photocopied, or otherwise—except for excerpts used in review, without the written permission of the publisher.

Printed in India at Pilgrims Press Ltd. Lalpur Varanasi

PILGRIMS PUBLISHING
◆ Varanasi ◆

THE WHITE GRASS PLAINS WILDLIFE RESERVE
Peter Byrne

Published by:
PILGRIMS PUBLISHING

An imprint of:
PILGRIMS BOOK HOUSE
(Distributors in India)
B 27/98 A-8, Nawabganj Road
Durga Kund, Varanasi-221010, India
Tel: 91-542-2314060,
Fax: 91-542-2312456
E-mail: pilgrims@satyam.net.in
Website: www.pilgrimsbooks.com

First Edition 2008
Copyright © 2008, Peter Byrne
All Rights Reserved

Layout & Cover design by Asha Mishra

ISBN: 978-81-7769-663-9
ISBN: 81-7769-663-7

The contents of this book may not be reproduced, stored or copied in any form—printed, electronic, photocopied, or otherwise—except for excerpts used in review, without the written permission of the publisher.

Printed in India at Pilgrim Press Pvt. Ltd. Lalpur Varanasi

A FIELD GUIDE
—to the mammals, reptiles, birds and fishes of the Sukila Phanta (White Grass Plains) Wildlife Reserve

The word 'sukila' is a Taru word. It means 'white'. The word 'phanta' is found in both the Nepalese and Taru languages. It means a 'plain'. In the autumn, every year, the grasses of the great central plain of this beautiful park seed, and then turn white. Hence its English name, The White Grass Plains, used in an abbreviated form, in this guidebook, as the WGP.

Contents

Introduction	ix
THE ELEPHANT	1
THE RHINOCEROS	5
THE CATS	9
THE LESSER CATS	18
THE BEARS	21
THE CIVETS	25
THE HYENAS	28
THE PANDAS	31
THE DEER	32
THE ANTELOPES	37
THE CANINES	40
THE SWINE	44
THE SAURIANS	47
THE APES, MONKEYS AND LEMURS	70
THE SNAKES	78
The Non-poisonous Snakes	78
The Poisonous Snakes	83
THE LIZARDS	86
THE TURTLES AND TORTOISES	93
THE HARES AND RABBITS	96
THE WEASELS	99
THE INSECTIVORES	104
THE PANGOLINS	107
THE MONGOOSES	109
THE RODENTS	112
THE BATS	143
THE BIRDS	151
THE FISHES	169
THE WHITE GRASS PLAINS WILDLIFE RESERVE	175
GLOSSARY	223
BIBLIOGRAPHY	228
ACKNOWLEDGEMENTS	231
ABOUT THE AUTHOR	234

INTRODUCTION

The White Grass Plains Wildlife Reserve is the jewel in the crown of Nepal's wildlife parks. Situated in the far southwest corner of the country, in an area which only in recent years has been opened to vehicular traffic, it consists of 200,000 acres of pristine forest, grassland and wetlands that provide habitat for a large variety of mammals, birds, reptiles and fishes. This guidebook contains, in addition to a detailed portrayal of the reserve itself, a listing and description of all of the species known to be presently living there. It also includes listings of animals which, because no studies have been done on the possibility of their being found within the park, and because their known distribution within the Indian subcontinent includes the Nepal Terai, and the WGP, may possibly be found there. With the exception of the birds and the fishes (see ACKNOWLEDGEMENTS) and photo credits, the listings, descriptions and photographs are the work of the author and are the result of his personal knowledge of the reserve, and his field experience within it, of more than fifty years.

THE ELEPHANT

THE ELEPHANT, *Elephas Maximus* (Linnaeus). Rana and Dangora Taru: *hatti*. Hindi: *hathi*, and, for females, *hathni*.

At one time, seven species of elephant existed in the Indian subcontinent. One of them was *Moreitherium*, a little creature that stood 42in in height. Today, one species of elephant survives there and throughout Asia, the Asian elephant. Males average 9ft at the shoulder, with females about a foot shorter. British hunting records from the days of the Raj list the largest male at 10ft 6in.

Nepal records list a single record male, a tusker, which I discovered and named in 1985. This was Tula Hatti, a giant pachyderm that stood 11ft at the shoulder. The shoulder height of elephants can be determined by measuring the diameter of a clear print of either forefoot and multiplying this by six. Tula Hatti's forefoot print had a diameter of 22in, which, multiplied by six, came to 132in, or 11ft. This made him not only the largest elephant in Nepal in his lifetime, but the largest in Asia of all time. This great animal divided his time between the WGP and the Bardia National Park and I saw him many times in the WGP over the last thirty years.

In 1998 this magnificent animal was killed by a poachers' bomb set in the Kheri district of Uttar Pradesh in India, a few miles southwest of the WGP. He had gone to Corbett Park with a group of elephants to eat bamboo and was returning to the WGP when he was killed, just a mile short of his home ground and the safety it offered.[1]

In the wild, the gestation period of the Asian elephant is seventeen months for a female birth, nineteen months for a male. Young are born one at a time and may stay with the mother, or with a group containing the mother, for all of their lives.

For many years the WGP has had a loose-knit herd of twenty elephants. At times they band together in a single group, but more often, probably depending on the availability of food, they break up into separate groups of from five to eight animals. In the past, each year and for many years, the herd would regularly leave the park in April and travel eastward along an ancient elephant walk that ran along the base of the hills, all the way to the forests of Bardia, where they spent the summer. In November they returned. In recent years they appear

---

[1] The bomb that Indian poachers use in the forests along the Indo-Nepal border to kill animals is composed of homemade, granulated gunpowder which, when compressed, ignites through abrasion and explodes. It is usually packed inside rotten fruit or vegetables and its principal target is deer or wild boar. Either species will nibble or bite on the fruit, or the vegetables, causing the gunpowder to explode; the animal's head is usually blown off, leaving the body for the poachers, who dry the meat and sell it commercially. Tula Hatti put his right front foot on one of these devilish devices and it was completely blown off. He staggered to a small pool in a semi-dry riverbed not far south of Pachui (near Kalkutta village) in Kailali district and stayed in the pool for five days before he died. Indian wildlife authorities, alerted to the animal's plight, could do nothing. But when he died they pulled his body out of the pool, using two farm tractors, and buried it near by. They also removed his tusks and took them away. For the full story of the tragic death of this great animal, see the reprint of my book, TULA HATTI, THE LAST GREAT ELEPHANT, first published by Faber & Faber, Manchester, N.H., which contains an epilogue describing his death; it is being published by Pilgrims Press, Katmandu, Nepal. In August 2006, two Sikhs from Palia Kalan, India, not far south of the Nepal border, one of them an ex-convict, admitted to being the poachers who prepared and set the bomb that killed Tula Hatti. No charges have been made against them and, political indifference in India to matters like this being what it is, it is doubtful if any will ever be made.

to have abandoned this annual migration. The reason is fairly obviously the resettlement of large numbers of hill people who, having lost their land to erosion and for other reasons, have been given new farmland in the area traversed by the ancient walk, effectively blocking it to the migration. Now most of the herd seem to stay in the park for all of the year, with the exception of a few that may venture west, from time to time, for a week or so, to the Corbett National Park in India.

I have always had a personal affinity with elephants, all the way back to a lovely old female named Lizzie, the property of the tea company I worked for in north Bengal in the fifties. I spent many hours on her back, exploring the Jaldaka River jungles of the western Dooars region, learning my jungle lore and enjoying every minute of it. Lizzie passed away somewhat tragically not long after I left the Dooars to live in Nepal. Torrential monsoon rains in lower Bhutan swelled the Jaldaka River, which in turned flooded the estate where I had lived for five years—Tondoo Tea Estate. The estate laborers, one thousand of them, men, women and children, took to the trees and stayed there until they were rescued. The principal rescuer was Lizzie, who apparently made hundreds of trips back and forth to high ground, carrying at times as many as twenty people on her back. The Indian army came in to help and eventually all but a few survived. But as the last people were being taken out, Lizzie, a grand old lady, just lay down and died, very possibly from exhaustion.

I have had many marvelous experiences with elephants in the WGP. These include having one—a wild elephant that we named Bump, because of a baseball-sized bump on the left side of his forehead—stand and watch me and allow me to walk up to within twenty paces of him, before turning quietly away. Another time I was charged by a young elephant, when I and my gun-bearer got too close to a herd and laughed so hard at the little fellow that he turned away and ran squealing back to his mother. On another occasion I had a female with a

The White Grass Plains

young one come right up to an open vehicle in which I was sitting, and then touch it with her trunk, as if to verify exactly what it was that she had encountered. And, illustrative of how incredibly quiet elephants can be when they move, the experience of having eighteen elephants walk past my tent in a camp on the Bauni River, all within fifty feet, on a very hot April afternoon, the sound of their passing no more than a whisper in the dry brown leaves of the early summer.

THE RHINOCEROS

THE GREAT INDIAN ONE-HORNED RHINOCEROS, *Rhinoceros unicornis* (Linnaeus). Taru: *gaira.* Nepalese: *gaida.* Hindi: *gonda* or *goonda.*

At one time, three species of rhinoceros were found in Asia. These were the Greater Onehorned Indian Rhinoceros, the Asiatic Two-horned Rhinoceros and the Smaller Onehorned, or Javan Rhinoceros. Now there may be only one left.

Until the end of the 1800s, the distribution of the Twohorned species, which, because of its coat of strong, wiry hairs, has also been unofficially known as the Hairy Rhinoceros, ranged from Assam all the way through Burma to Indo-China, Malaysia, Borneo and Sumatra. As of about 1980, it was believed that there were probably no more than twenty or thirty left in the wild. As this figure, from a quarter of a century ago, would be less than the biological minimum needed to sustain the species, it is not unreasonable to presume it is now extinct. The principal reason for its demise, if it is gone, would be poaching, mainly for its horns, but also for nearly all of its other body parts, believed by ignorant indigenous people to have medicinal or even magical powers.

The Javan rhinoceros may well have suffered the same unhappy fate. At 5ft 10in at the shoulder and a little larger than the Twohorned, it once ranged all the way from Bengal to Sumatra.

Again, like the Two-horned, superstition and ignorance and, one would believe, political indifference, has brought about what may well be the extinction of the species. A survey was carried out in 1960 in the one place where it appeared a few of them were left—the Udjung Kulon Sanctuary, situated at the far western end of Java. The result was a count of about thirty animals. In the time span between 1960 and now, some forty-seven years, it seems doubtful that the species could have survived.

Now, in the new century, we are left with but one species of rhino in Asia. This is the Greater One-horned, a huge animal that is bigger in height and bulk than the African Black Rhino. Males will stand 6ft at the shoulder with a body circumference, behind the withers, of 11ft. The single horn, which is actually not horn at all, but compressed and solidified hair, is usually about 8in in length—an old British record, from Assam, records one of 24in. The animal is solitary, usually meeting only to mate. Females attain sexual maturity in four years and males in seven. The period of gestation is about sixteen months.

Rhinos frequented western Nepal until the turn of the century. Then they were exterminated through hunting and poaching. The last one in the forests of Kanchanpur—the district that contains the WGP—was shot by a British hunter named Drummond, from Tanakpur, in 1910.

In the 1990s, working in the WGP on a conservation project, I came across prints of a lone rhino in the Rani Tal area. The find was reported to the WGP game warden of that time, who stated emphatically that there were no rhinos in the park and that the prints were obviously of something else. I subsequently tracked and photographed a single animal, which, it is believed, must have wandered into the park from the Indian forests of the Pilibhit area, to the south. (Coming from these forests into Nepal must have meant passing through Indian agricultural land, with villages, dogs and people—ignorant peasants to whom all wild creatures mean nothing but food. How the animal survived this without being killed is something of a miracle.)

Later I approached the Nepalese government with a proposal that some additional animals be transferred from Chitwan National Park, where they are plentiful, to the WGP. This was agreed, and in November 2000 six animals, two males and four females, were successfully transferred to the WGP. Since that time two of the females have given birth, bringing the numbers of the present rhino group of the WGP to nine animals. One of the animals that gave birth was the one I had first discovered in the WGP; plans are now (2006) in the works to transfer more.

In the WGP the best places to find rhinos are in the wetlands around Rani Tal, in the Great Swamp—the Andaneha—in the Lal Mutti area, in the Sal Gaudi Tal swamp and also in the dense and almost primeval jungles that lie immediately to the north of Sal Gaudi Tal.

For the amateur naturalist, rhinos are best viewed from elephant-back. One reason is the dense and swampy nature of where they live, terrain that is often very difficult to penetrate and travel through on foot. Another is that the rhino is a short-tempered and cantankerous beast, very easy to provoke and sometimes quite dangerous when disturbed. Females with young are to be avoided at all times, for they will not hesitate to attack a person on foot and will even take on an elephant.

In an attack on a person, they will seldom use the horn, which is essentially a digging tool, but will bite, with sometimes dire consequences for the victim. Some years ago a researcher from Minneapolis, Dave Smith, had the misfortune to unexpectedly encounter one in the Chitwan forests in central Nepal. Walking into the forest in the early morning with his young son, and trailed by a villager, he did not notice a sleeping rhino lying by the side of the trail. The animal woke up and immediately charged. The villager grabbed the boy and ran; the rhino then concentrated its attention on Dave. It bit him, very nastily, thirteen times and only stopped when another rhino appeared, whereupon the two of them walked away together. Dave survived, but his accident should be viewed as an object lesson for anyone thinking about going on foot into jungle that contains these massive and dangerous animals, especially in WGP.

The animal is extraordinary in appearance, with what looks like armor plate for a hide, with metal rivets holding it together. Being extraordinary, it also naturally follows that it will have some unique habits. One of these is connected with one of its primary natural functions, defecation. When the animal feels a need to defecate, which I understand is once a day and usually in the early evening, it almost always goes to the same place to do this. It continues doing it there until the pile of droppings may reach a height of four feet. A pile this high will eventually become inconvenient and uncomfortable to use, so when it reaches these proportions the animal will start another pile somewhere else. As if that were not odd enough, it compounds the oddity by always approaching its pile backwards, something, sadly, that makes it vulnerable to poachers, who dig a pit under the pile and camouflage it with dung. When the animal falls in, it is quickly and brutally speared to death.

In early 2005 a single female was found dead in the *phantas*, close to the main east-west road, about one and half miles west of the Bauni bridge. An autopsy revealed a seven-month-old fetus and also the fact that the mother's stomach contained a mass of worms, the latter most probably being the cause of her death. In 2006 another female was found dead, of unknown but what appeared to be natural causes. Presently there are between eight and ten rhinos in the WGP, a delightful outcome of my finding of a single animal, the Lone Rhino, as she was called, the first in almost a hundred years in the far west forests.

THE CATS

THE TIGER, *Panthera tigris* (Linnaeus). Rana Taru: *bagta*. Dangora Taru: *bagh*. Nepalese: *seer*. Hindi: *bagh*.

An average male tiger measures 9ft–9ft 6in. Females average 8ft–8ft 6in. The average weight for males is 375–425lbs, and for females, 275–325lbs. The big cat is a solitary animal, only associating when mating. The gestation period in the wild is about thirteen weeks. Two cubs is the average number born and they will stay with the mother for up to three years, during which time the female will not mate.

The tiger is the greatest of the cats and in the WGP it is the dominant feline. There have been tigers in the area since at least 1895 and probably long before that. Lord Baden Powell, hunting with fellow British military officers in the WGP in the summer of 1895, reported tigers as very numerous and, over the course of a three-week safari, hunting from elephant-back, he and his fellow hunters shot six.

In 1953, when I first went into the WGP, there were large numbers of tigers living there. I was not able to do any counts at that time, but from the signs—pug marks and the remains of kills—it would be safe to say that they were at capacity for the size of the area.

The WGP has produced some very big tigers over the years. In the days before conservation studies, all measurements and weights that were recorded were of course as result of hunting. The largest taken during my hunting years measured 10ft

3in and was taken by a safari client, William Holmes, an American sportsman from Los Angeles. Its weight was 496lbs.

Reliable records of tiger hunting in north India and Nepal indicate tigers of up to eleven feet and possibly more. The largest tiger ever taken, weighed and measured by senior British officials at the time, was a male shot by a Mrs. Laurie Johnson in the Dooars district of north Bengal, the area, many years later, where I was a tea planter. The date was some time in the late 1800s and the occasion was a hunt, probably a beat, during the course of which Mrs. Johnson, who is believed to have been the wife of a tea planter, bagged the huge cat. The official measurement, verified by senior British officials and also by the esteemed author, W. S. Burke, in his book, THE INDIAN FIELD SHIKAR BOOK, who were present at the hunt, was twelve feet six inches.

In the WGP, tigers tend to make their habitat close to wherever water is available and, being essentially shy and secretive animals, they prefer dense cover whenever possible. As a result, the principal tiger habitat of the park is to be found close to the five rivers that are the main water sources. These are the Sarda to the west, the Bauni in the center, the Gobria and the Chaundar to the east, and the Hagania, which is the feeder river of the parks principal lake, Rani Tal. Of all of these areas, the jungles through which the Bauni runs provide the most attractive tiger habitat, because, unlike the Chaundar, the Gobria and the Sarda, with their park boundary village populations, it is more secluded. Another area which holds tigers includes the small islands of the Andaneha, the Great Swamp of the WGP. Its principal attraction for tigers is probably its deep, muddy-bottomed waters and dense stands of elephant grass, which make human access to its interior difficult to nearly impossible. There also may be small dry islands in the Andaneha that would provide comfortable lairs. I have climbed trees at the edge of the Andaneha, and using binoculars, have made a visual search. Small clumps of trees far out in the dense brush and muddy waters of the swamp indicate this possibility.

In 2005 the WGP had a population of not less than thirty tigers. Their principal food is the *cheetal*, or Spotted Deer, and Swamp Deer, followed by Wild Boar and Hog Deer. They will also take large domestic animals like cows and buffalo that may stray into the park; a kill that I found in the central grasslands in 1980 contained the remains of a horse, including two of its metal shoes, the animal no doubt a stray from one of the park's border villages.

In any discussion of tigers, of course, comes the question of man-eaters. Thus it seems fitting to look at the WGP's record of man-eaters through the known records of its history. It can be dealt with fairly quickly because, even though the district which contains the park, Kanchanpur, borders on to Kumaon, in India—an area which has produced a dozen ferocious man-eaters over the years, including the most famous and deadly of them all, the man-eating tiger of Rupal Champawat—the number of man-eaters known to have actually operated in the park is limited.

When I first came to the WGP in 1953, inquiries were conducted about man-eaters with the Tarus of Haria, Singpur, Balma and Barcola. The information that was forthcoming was a little vague. Yes, Taru villagers had been attacked and killed by tigers from time to time. But whether the attacking cats were man-eaters, or just cats provoked to attack by unusual circumstances, was difficult to definitely determine. Some people, I was told, had been eaten after being killed. But not all.

During my hunting years, I had a keen interest in man-eaters and one day hoped to hunt one. Eventually an opportunity came, though not in the WGP. The man-eater in question was operating in the Girwa Kauriala delta, about 75 miles east of the WGP in Bardia, where it had killed and eaten forty villagers. The story of what turned out to be quite a dramatic hunt is recounted in my book, *GONE ARE THE DAYS*, published by Safari Press, Huntington Beach, California.

In November 1999, a tigress with two six-month-old cubs attacked and killed a villager in the grasslands of the one time village of Haria. After killing the man, the cat and her cubs ate most of him. In December 1999 the same tigress killed again, this time the victim being a Taru named Mangal, who was my camp cook. The victim was taken at night while riding his bicycle back from the village of Immelia, on the edge of the reserve, where he had gone to visit friends. Attacked from behind, he was severely bitten on the head and almost certainly killed instantly. After killing him, the tigress dragged his body a hundred yards into thick grass where, under a small tree, she and the cubs ate parts of his body—the flesh from the backs of his legs and from his chest and all of his left arm, with his wristwatch.

I was able to track the tigress and, using a motion sensor camera, set up a camera trap on a trail that she was using close to the lake of Rani Tal. The rare photograph obtained is the only one ever taken of a living man-eater. It appears here. After killing the cook, the tigress seems to have gone back to killing natural prey and there were no more human fatalities for some time. The next recorded fatality, again of a Taru villager, was on Sunday 06 February 2005.

As to the present status of the tigers of the WGP—thanks to the diligent and energetic work of Nepal's Department of National Parks and Wildlife, and the protection afforded by the roving, field patrols of the Nepal Army, the tigers of the WGP seem to be maintaining a reasonably healthy balance.

THE LEOPARD, *Panthera pardus* (Linnaeus). Rana Taru: *chota bagh*. Nepalese: *cheetua*. Hindi: *sona chita*.

Male leopards, with their tails, average 7ft; females about 6ft. Males will weigh about 140–150lbs and females 100–120lbs.

The Cats

The largest leopard taken during my hunting years in the WGP, shot by a safari client, a Mrs. Sally McConnell, of Red Bluff, California, measured 7ft 6in and weighed 165lbs.

The coloration of the leopard is a dark yellow under a pattern of markings that are often described as spots, but which are actually beautiful, black rosettes. The only places the Asian leopard has spots are on the neck, chest and upper legs.

Like the tiger, the leopard is a solitary animal, meeting other members of its species only to mate. Mating is believed to be throughout the year. Females will produce young from the age of two and a half; the gestation period in the wild is about 90 days. Usually, two cubs are born at a time, though as many as four have been recorded; the cubs are weaned after four months. The food of the leopard is essentially anything that it can overpower and kill. Its principal food in the WGP is deer, all of the species with perhaps the exception of Sambar and Swamp deer—these two animals, because of their excessive weight and bulk, are too physically difficult for this smaller cat to pull down and kill.

The leopard is truly one of the most beautiful of the cats. Seen in its natural surroundings, in the dapped light of the *sal* forest, or standing in the dark green grass of the WGP *phantas*, there are few sights more splendid. In movement the animal is a phantom, silent as a shadow, and in motion seeming to almost float above the ground. In strength it is unsurpassed, being possibly, according to Jim Corbett, one of the strongest animals in the world for its size. (Corbett records one, a man-eater, carrying a villager, a man of average weight—probably about 130lbs—for two miles without putting him down.)

Few people get to see the agility and the incredible dexterity with which a leopard can place its feet and move through the densest brush like a ghost. I have been fortunate to personally experience this in the Terai and also under domestic circumstances.

The White Grass Plains

When I was a tea planter in north Bengal, in the 1940s, I had two leopards as pets; they lived with me for a number of years. One was from the Jaldaka forests of the Dooars district, the other from Bhutan. One time, as an experiment, and to entertain guests, I placed fifteen wine glasses on the polished surface of a large dining table, each about 4in apart. My Bhutanese leopard, at this time three-quarters grown, was picked up and then carefully lowered, feet first, to stand into the middle of the set of glasses. Not only did it walk through them without touching a single one, but its tail did the same, winding through the glasses and following the flowing line of its body with a delicacy that was magical to watch. My Jaldaka cat had equal abilities, one of which, when it was feeling playful, was to leap up and bounce off my dining room walls, 8–10ft up, and then flip over backwards to land on its feet.[2]

The White Grass Plains has a relatively small population of leopards. This is most probably because of the comparatively large population of tigers. All big cats are highly territorial and tigers will not tolerate leopards in their territories. When they meet, if the leopard does not instantly flee, a tiger, male

---

[2] My two pet leopards lived with me for two years. They were very even-tempered and friendly animals and, as long as their needs were supplied—food, water and a place to sleep—they made great pets. They lived with me in my planter bungalow, free to come and go as they pleased, but sleeping inside at night; probably as a result of this my bungalow was one of the few in the district that was never burgled. I trained both animals as retrievers, shooting pigeons, doves and jungle fowl for them to retrieve, the only difference between them and a good canine retriever being that they were not prepared to give up whatever it was they got their teeth into. Birds they ate on the spot, but only after carefully plucking the feathers out by mouth, holding the carcasses between their front paws. One of the animals walked into the forest one day and disappeared. It probably fell victim to a tiger, or perhaps walked into a village, expecting people to be friendly; its end there would been quick and on the points of spears. The other was given to the Taronga Park Zoo in Sydney, Australia, where it lived happily for many years.

or female, will attack it. Across the years I have found the carcasses of three leopards killed by tigers.

One of these was in the forest just north of the Singpur guard post. The report of a kill came in the early morning, and when I got to the scene, the park warden of that time, a myopic gentleman with little love for his post and minimal interest in wildlife, had already arrived. Taking one nervous look at the dead cat and at a dark red hole in the top of its head, he said that it was obvious that it had been shot and that a poacher was to blame; he then gave instructions for the body of the cat to be taken to park headquarters for burial and departed hastily for the comfort and safety of his office.

After he left and before the body was removed, I made a thorough examination of the scene. Carefully reading the ground signs, in the brush where the dead cat lay and also in the dust of a nearby trail, I came to a conclusion that was quite different from that of the little bureaucrat.

In the early morning, just after dawn, the leopard, probably returning from a night of hunting, encountered a big tigress. The smaller cat instantly turned and fled. The tigress, however, was equally quick and launched an immediate attack. Assessing the success of flight as being somewhat remote, the leopard changed its mind and, racing to a big fig tree, flung itself at the bole and began to claw its way up. It managed to get about 6ft or 7ft up the tree. A little higher and it would have been safe, for whereas leopards are skilful climbers, tigers seldom climb trees. But the tigress was close behind, close enough to reach upwards and grab the leopard by the rump and drag it from the tree.

The desperate and futile attempts of the leopard to hold on to the tree and escape its attacker were indicated by the long, deep claw marks it left in the bark as the tigress pulled it down. A short, fierce struggle ensued, clearly indicated by the minute spots of blood on the leaves of surrounding bushes, some of them more than 4ft above the ground. Then the tigress got the leopard's head in its jaws and sunk a canine tooth into its brain. The smaller cat died instantly and the tigress then walked away, leaving it where it was.

The WGP may have as many as twenty leopards living in the park at this time, 2007. Unlike the tiger, the leopard needs little cover and will even make a lair in dry *nullahs* with little vegetation. If undisturbed, it will remain in the same habitat for many years. At the same of writing, one has lived in a dry *nullah* close to one of my permanent camps on the Bauni for more than ten years; it uses the Bauni bridge to go hunting in the central forests and has been seen and photographed, crossing the bridge, several times. The future of the leopard is a little more promising than that of the tiger. Like tigers, leopards are hunted by poachers for their body parts, which are used by ignorant people for both medicinal and aphrodisiacal purposes. But because of their smaller size, their stealth, their need for little cover and their ability to survive, undetected, close to human habitation, they will probably long outlive their larger cousin.

Although the Indian territories of Kumaon and Garhwal, not far west of the WGP, have produced several man-eating leopards across the years, including the fearsome beast that, with four hundred human kills to its credit, was known as the Panar Man-eater, there is no record of man-eating leopards in the WGP during my time there, which to date covers more than fifty years.

THE CLOUDED LEOPARD, *Neofelis nebulosa* (Griffith). Taru: *unknown*. Nepalese: *amchitd*.

The Clouded Leopard is noted for its quite beautiful body markings, which resemble black flowers on a gold background. The face is marked with cheek stripes and the head is spotted. Males average about 6ft and will weigh 40–45lbs. It is nocturnal and preys mainly upon small animals; like the leopard, it will eat anything it can overpower. Unlike the leopard, it is mainly arboreal; females will give birth to their young in hollow tree trunks, high off the ground.

The Cats

The Taru people of the far west Terai do not seem to know this animal; this may be because it has become very rare in recent years. In five decades of camping in the Terai I have seen only one, in the WGP, while hunting with a Mr. Charles Rose of Pensacola, Florida in 1960. There appear to be none in the WGP now; some experts seem to think that the animal may be extinct in Nepal.

ASIAN LION and ASIAN CHEETAH

These two other big cats may have lived in the WGP many years ago. The Taru people who lived in the park when I first went there had a name for the lion—Sher Baba—and they knew what it meant. They did not, however, know of the cheetah, or recognize pictures of it. Today, a small group of Asian lions lives in an area called the Gir Forest, north of Bombay in India, where their food seems to be mainly domestic cattle; their hopes for survival are meager. The Asian cheetah is now extinct. In 1957 the Maharaja of Baroda showed me two semi-domesticated cheetah that that he kept for hunting Black Buck antelope. These may have been the last of the species in India.

SNOW LEOPARD

Although not found in the WGP, Nepal has one other large cat that deserves mention; this is the Snow Leopard. It is a little smaller than the common leopard of the Terai, averaging, with its tail, about 6ft in length. Its habitat is the high ranges of the Himalaya, from Kashmir to Bhutan. It is seldom found below 10,000 feet.

THE LESSER CATS

The Indo-Nepal region has a number of what are known as 'lesser cats'. These include the Desert Cat, the Fishing Cat, the Golden Cat, the Jungle Cat, the Leopard Cat, the Marbled Cat, the Pallas's Cat and the Rusty Spotted Cat. Of these, five, as follows, can be found in the WGP.

THE MARBLED CAT, *Felis marmorata* (Martin). Rana Taru: *jungli billi.*

The Marbled Cat has a body of about 18in and a tail of the same length. Its body is generally marbled in coloration, with stripes on the head and neck and spots on the limbs and tail. Like the Clouded Leopard, it is believed to be arboreal and its prey is probably mostly rodents and other small animals and birds. Because of its extreme shyness and nocturnal habits, very little is known about this animal, or about its survival status. The WGP may have a few, although personally I have never seen one.

THE GOLDEN CAT, *Felis temmincki* (Vigors & Horsfield). Rana Taru: *jungle billi.*

The Golden Cat is uniformly gold in color, with the exception of the face and head, which carries some markings, including a stripe on the inner side of the eye, which separates and continues to the crown. Its average length is 4ft, of which 1ft 6in will be the tail. Very little is known about the habits of the

Golden Cat and, if it is to be found in the WGP, which is possible, it might well be in very small numbers.

THE LEOPARD CAT, *Felis bengalensis* (Kerr). Rana Taru: *chota billi* or *chota cheetua*. Hindi: *chita billi*.

The Leopard Cat is so called because its coloration and markings make it appear like a small leopard. It is about the size of a European domestic cat, with the tail about half the length of the body. It has been seen in the WGP and is known to the Taru people of the area. However, they have no special name for it, calling it simply a 'jungle cat', and often, in the dappled light of the forest, mistaking it for a small panther. The animal is nocturnal, like so many of the cats, and its food is any animal that is smaller than itself and thus susceptible to attack. It will make a lair in a hollow tree, off the ground; this suggests that it may also hunt in trees at night for roosting birds.

THE JUNGLE CAT, *Felis chaus* (Guldenstaedt). Rana and Dangora Taru: *jungle billi*. Hindi: *jungli billi*.

In the WGP the Jungle Cat appears to be the most common of the smaller cats. Including the tail, it measures about 3ft in length; adults will weigh about 7lbs. It is like a domestic cat in appearance but with longer legs. Its coloration is a yellowish gray. The ears are chestnut and tipped with tufts of black hair. The tail has black rings and is tipped with black; its food is birds and small animals. Like the Leopard Cat, it will lie up in hollow trees. It is very fast in pursuit and attack and thus capable of taking most small mammals with ease.

THE FISHING CAT, *Felis viverrina* (Bennett). Rana and Dangora Taru: *macha kani billi*.

The Fishing Cat is one of the larger of the small cats. It measures up to 4ft in length (including the tail) and can weight as

The White Grass Plains

much as 25lbs. It is stocky in build and is covered with short, coarse fur, especially designed, one would believe, to shed water. Its coloration is gray with brown undertones. Like some of the other small cats, as part of its natural camouflage it has dark lines running from the top of the head to the shoulders, where these break into bars and spots. Its habitat is usually close to water; it will be found in swamps and, in the WGP, most probably in the Andaneha. Its name might suggest that it actually goes in the water and pursues fish by swimming and diving for them. This is not quite true. Its diet does include fish, but it catches them by waiting for them on an overhanging bank or partially waterlogged tree and, when they come within reach, scooping them out of the water with a lightning fast movement of the paw. Its diet also includes mollusks.

NOTE: Five other species of lesser cat are found within the Indian subcontinent. These are the DESERT CAT, THE CARACAL, THE LYNX, THE PALLAS'S CAT AND THE RUSTY-SPOTTED CAT. None of these have been identified in the WGP.

THE BEARS

Asia has a number of species of bear. They include the Brown, the Malay, the Red, the Himalayan Black and the Sloth. Of these, the author has identified two in the WGP—the Sloth and the Himalayan Black. The others, because of this known distribution, are hardly likely to be found there.

THE SLOTH BEAR, *Melarsus ursinus* (Shaw). Rana and Dangora Taru: *balua*. Hindi: *bhalu*.

The Sloth Bear is usually recognized by its wild matt of thick hair, its long muzzle and its under-hung lower lip. It is a big animal as animals go in the Indo-Nepal Terai, but, as a bear, nothing like its North American cousins, the Grizzly and the Brown. In size it will measure 4.5–5.5ft, standing 26in at the shoulder. Males can weigh up to 320lbs and females less, averaging about 150lbs. Some but not all have a white V-shaped insignia on the chest; the ends of the feet are off-white or yellowish in color. The claws are white and longer in the forefoot than in the hind. Its hair is black but with brown overtones; in some cases almost totally brown.

Within its known ranges, the forests of India, from the edge of the Himalaya into Assam, and south to Sri Lanka, the Sloth will be found just about anywhere an available food supply will support it. Though mostly but not everywhere nocturnal, the author has seen them foraging for food during daylight

The White Grass Plains

hours. Like other animals, including the tiger, human activity, or the lack of it, will shape the measure of this habit.

Like all bears, in eating habits the Sloth is an animal which is about to eat, is eating, or has just finished eating and is thinking about eating again. Their lives revolve around food and the need to find it, for they are animals with voracious appetites. Their search for food may require them to travel considerable distances. It certainly compels them to work hard to find the fruit, both wild and domestic, which is part of their diet.

Surprisingly for such a large animal, they also eat insects, among which are the larvae of termites. Like the pangolin, they will tear into a termite mound, usually half-destroying it in the process. They also dig out and eat the grubs of dung beetles, for which they may have to dig down as much as four feet. Honey is also a food for the Sloth. They look for the giant combs of both the rock bee and the forest bee, climb up, smash the comb off with a swing of a powerful paw and then return to the ground to eat it, their thick hair coat protecting them from the thousands of enraged bees that this action will generate. Flowers are also eaten, including the petals of the silk cotton tree when these bloom and fall to the ground. And of course domestic crops, including sugar cane, maize and date palms; when the latter are tapped by villagers for toddy, the Sloth will climb up and drink this from the earthen pot set to collect it.

The Sloth mates during the monsoon. Females give birth in December and January; the cubs may stay with the mother for as long as three years. The cubs travel with their mother on feeding forays, riding on her back and hanging on for dear life with their little claws buried in her coarse fur coat. . Mothers with young are dangerously quick to provoke and show a savage nature in attack. They are responsible for many injuries and even deaths among native peoples, possibly more than any other wild animal in Asia.

The Bears

THE HIMALAYAN BLACK BEAR, Selanarctus thibetanus (G. Cuvier). Rana and Dangora Taru: *balu*. Sherpa, *thom*. Hindi: *reech, rinch, bhalu*.

The Black Bear has a range that takes it from the Terai to high in the Himalaya. I have seen one at 12,000 feet in the upper Arun River valley. I later rescued some cubs, the offspring of a mother who had been trapped and killed by Sherpa hunters at 10,000 feet in the upper Iswa Khola, in the central east Nepal Himalaya.

Close in size to its Indian cousin, the Sloth Bear, adult male Black Bears measure up to 5ft 5in, with females just a little less. What distinguishes it from the Sloth is its smooth coat and black claws. In coloration it is black, with a brown muzzle and a white chin. Again, like the Sloth, it has the white chest V, but in the Black this may vary from white to yellow, or even buff.

The Black migrates to some extent in winter and this habit, no doubt shaped by climate and food needs, is what takes it from the bleak ranges of the upper Himalayan foothills down to the Terai. The animal is essentially nocturnal; when inactive it will spend the day in a rock cave or in the hollow of a tree. However, as with certain other animals, this habit is shaped by the proximity of people and their movements, and adjusted accordingly. In isolated areas free of human habitation and activity, and certainly if the animal is hungry, it will not hesitate to forage in daylight hours.

The Black is an omnivore and, though its principal diet consists of fruit, berries, insects like termites, and honey, being an omnivore—or just being a bear—it will eat anything, including the carrion of all kinds of animals and fish. My four cubs, who lived with me for a year, ate everything that was put in front of them. They were mostly fed oatmeal with yak or cow milk, but they also enjoyed eating shoes, gloves, woolen hats and leather belts. Introduced to a Himalayan wild raspberry bush and fed one raspberry each as an introduction, they quickly learned to strip the branches of the fruit. The same applied to ground-growing Himalayan wild strawberries; when they had finished with a patch, it looked as though it had been vacuumed.[3]

Being an omnivore, part of the diet of the Black includes animal flesh. It will not hesitate to kill any animal that it thinks it can overpower, including of course domestic animals like sheep and goats. They have been known to attack cattle. No doubt in the wild, deer and wild boar would be part of their diet if they were capable of catching them.

The Black is a very aggressive animal and, driven by hunger, can be fearless. They will drive a leopard off its kill and have been known on rare occasions to do the same thing with tigers. They are capable of powerful, ear-splitting screams, and the psychological effect of this on a big cat, coupled with an aggressive attack, will sometimes put it to flight.

Like the Sloth, with its short temper and disagreeable disposition, the Black is very easy to provoke. The result is many documented attacks on humans, usually people who accidentally stumble on the animal while it is feeding, or upon a female with cubs. The attack is usually a short, snarling rush at the object of the animal's ire, with the bear then rising up to seize the person by the shoulders and bite into the face. I have seen the dreadful injuries that this behavior produces—shoulders raked and pock-marked with the deep wounds of the claws, faces twisted and destroyed by the dreadful bites. We do not know which bear is responsible for the most attacks, the most injuries or deaths of humans, but it may well be the Black.

---

[3] For the interest of readers, the author's four bears eventually went to zoos. Two to the San Antonio Zoological Gardens in San Antonio, Texas, and two to the Taronga Park Zoo in Sydney, Australia. All four lived long and happy lives, and in the process, probably because of the TLC they received while young, became great pets of their keepers.

THE CIVETS

THE LARGE INDIAN CIVET, *Viverra zibetha* (Linnaeus). Dangora Taru: *ningal bagh*. Nepalese: *bhran*. Hindi: *kattas*.

The Large Indian Civet is a sturdily built member of the order *Viverridea*, its nearest relative being the cat. It has short, strong legs and an elongated body. The shoulders, chest and tail are ornamented with black and white bands; the body, which has a thick black band running down the center of the back, is covered with broken, zigzag, vertical lines. Adults measure 2ft 6in, and males and females are about the same size.

The animal is nocturnal, lying up in the daytime in thick scrub or dense grass. Its food consists of small animals, birds, frogs, lizards and crabs. However, it is an omnivore and will also eat berries, fruits and vegetables. It is reasonably common in the WGP, though mostly around the boundaries, suggesting that it might also take an interest in the domestic fowl of the villagers that surround the park. At the author's hunting camps on the Bauni River, there were always civets around at night, getting into the trash cans and exploring the camp kitchen. In the Dooars district of north Bengal, where I spent several years, it was very common and many were killed by trucks and cars on the highways.

THE SMALL INDIAN CIVET, *Viverricula indica* (Desmarest). Taru: *ningal bagh*. Hindi: *kasturi*.

The Small Indian Civet is smaller than its cousin, the Large Indian Civet. An adult male will measure 2ft, with a tail of about 1ft. This lesser member of the civet family does not have the black back-band of its larger cousin, and while its body markings on the head, chest and tail, are similar, the principal patterns of the body are long, thin stripes above and, on either side, large spots. Its coloration is a greenish brown.

The animal prefers long grass or scrub in which to make its lair; it seems to stay out of dense forest. Its food consists of rats and mice, lizards, birds, frogs and large insects. It is fairly common in the border areas of the WGP, and the Taru people, not given to acute distinction between animals that look alike, give it the same name as the Large Indian Civet.

THE COMMON PALM CIVET, or TODDY CAT, *Paradoxurus hermaphroditus* (Pallas). Rana Taru: *bund bilai*. Hindi: *lakati*.

The Toddy Cat is a dark brown civet, with long, rough hair. It has four white facial patches, one below each eye and one on either side of the nose. Adults measure about 2ft in length, with a tail of about 12in; the weight averages 8–10lbs.

The animals are essentially forest dwellers and are mainly arboreal. But the constant search for food brings them down from the trees, so they also hunt on the ground. The Taru people of the villages surrounding the WGP say that they nest in the roofs of their houses. In the WGP a campsite with its attendant organic waste—fruit and vegetable peelings—seems to attract them.

Their principal food is small mammals and birds, mice and rats; but they will also eat fruit, in season. The name Toddy Cat derives from their habit of drinking the toddy, the juice that exudes from palm trees, when these are tapped and potted by villagers for use as an alcoholic beverage.

The young are born throughout the year, in litters of three to four.

The Civets

THE SPOTTED LINSANG or TIGER CIVET, Prionodon pardicolor *(Hodgson)*.

The Tiger Civet measures about 30in in length and weighs about 2lbs. Its bold coloration—a large black band running down the sides, the body spotted with large, distinctive spots, and its banded tail—distinguish it from all of the other civets. It has been seen in the WGP. A shy and secretive animal, little is known of its breeding habits. It is both terrestrial and arboreal. Its prey is birds and small mammals.

THE BINTURONG or BEAR CAT, *Arctitus binturong* (Raffles). Taru: names unknown. Hindi: *yung*.

The Binturong is also a member of the civet family; its distribution includes the Terai of Nepal. It measures about 2ft 6in in length, with a tail of 24in. The animal has tufted ears and a rough, coarse-haired coat, which make it look almost like a small bear. It has a very thickly-haired and prehensile tail. It is black in color but with dashes of white and buff.

This civet is a creature of the deep forest and is mainly arboreal. It is nocturnal in its hunting. It is omnivorous and its food will include small animals like mice, lizards, and birds. A very shy and secretive animal, little seems to be known about its breeding, its gestation period, or the number of young produced in a litter. The author has not seen one in the WGP, but because its general distribution includes the Nepal Terai, it could be found there.

One other species of civet is to be found in the Indo-Nepal region. This is the HIMALAYAN PALM CIVET, an animal of the hill forests. To the best of my knowledge, it is not found in the WGP.

THE HYENAS

THE STRIPED HYENA, *Hyaena hyaena* (Linnaeus). Rana Taru: *lochria,* or *har har.* Dangora Taru: *bowasa.* Hindi: *hundar* or *lakkar bagha.*

The hyena found throughout the Indian subcontinent, including the Terai forests of Nepal, is the Striped Hyena. The animal is doglike in appearance, with a large head and well-muscled shoulders, the latter being ridged with a dorsal crest of thick, wiry hair. From the front, the body slopes back to what appear to be underdeveloped hindquarters. The ears, carried on its broad doglike head, are large, pointed and upright. Its coloration varies with the season, from a cold-weather coat that is a tawny cream to a dusty off-white during the hot days of the monsoon.

Adult males will measure—inclusive of the animal's short tail—up to 5ft in length, with a height at the shoulder of about 3ft and a weight of about 85lbs. Females are slightly smaller. The animal's pugmarks are distinctive, similar to that of a dog, except that the forefoot imprint is much larger than that of the hind foot, in addition to which the imprint of the main pad is oval in shape.

The animal is mostly nocturnal, certainly so where there is human habitation and human diurnal movement. As such, it spends its days in hiding, preferably in what is its desired den, small caves or holes in the banks of secluded *nullahs*. It lives in small groups or in pairs; single individuals are seldom seen. It is basically a scavenger and is designed by nature as such, seeking as its food the carcasses of animals that have died of natural causes or been killed by predators. In many cases this will mean that the predator animal that made the kill has eaten its fill, leaving, with the added attention of vultures and other scavengers, very little more than the bones. But these are what the hyena regards as food and, to allow for this, nature has provided it with massive jaw muscles and powerful, bone-crushing teeth. It is said that a mature hyena can break up the leg bones of a dead elephant; certainly the massive leg and rib bones of something as large as a domestic buffalo, a two thousand pound animal, are no obstacle to its dining needs. The animal's feces, when found, are a clear indication of diet, usually being near-white in color with the calcium content of consumed animal bone, and often containing semi-digested chunks of bone as large as a golf ball.

However, though designed as a scavenger, the hyena is also a hunter. Among its prey are pariah dogs that are foolish enough to wander out of the village at night. The method of hunting probably consists of initial contact via the hyena's sense of smell, which is acute in the animal, a slow and careful stalk to get close to the target animal, and then a short, fast rush culminating in a single, fatal bite to a vital part of the chosen prey. The prey will then be picked up and carried to a secluded place to be devoured, or to the hyena's den, the latter being more likely if there are pups. When I first went into the WGP in the fifties, two hyenas had a den in a big hole in the base of the vertical bank of a *nullah*, close to my camp on the rise of ground just north of the Bauni bridge. Inspecting it, I found and counted the skulls of twenty village dogs that had been brought there to be eaten.

The hyena is not believed to be dangerous to man, preferring to avoid humans whenever possible. However, there are authenticated records of attacks on humans in India and the British Raj hunter-author, Lt.-Col. R. W. Burton, writes of having shot a hyena that had killed and eaten a woman.

The White Grass Plains

Hunting in the WGP, years ago, I encountered hyenas several times in the early morning and late evening. Once, returning to camp on foot in the late evening and carrying on my shoulder a peafowl that I had just bagged for dinner, I found a large male following me, very probably attracted by the odor of the big dead bird. Each time I stopped and turned around to look at it, the animal stopped and stood and watched me and this continued for about half a mile. Then, when the massively-jawed animal started getting closer—and eventually, with the light fading, a little too close for my liking—I fired a warning shot over its head that sent it scampering off.

So are hyenas dangerous to man? Apart from very isolated instances of attacks on man, I do not think so. When I lived in north Bengal in the forties, several of my tea planter friends had hyena pets. They were docile and friendly animals, they were easily housetrained and they were generally regarded as being very safe with children.

In the 1950s and 1960s, hyenas were reasonably common in the WGP. Every evening after dark their calls would mingle with those of the jackals and foxes, their distinctive but eerie laughing chatter echoing through the damp air of the winter night. Now—2007—and for the last decade, I have seen no sign of any in the reserve, heard no calls at night, nor found any spoor on the jungle roads. I do not know the reason for this. The principal enemy of the animal would obviously be the leopard, with which it would be obliged to share the hunting night. But the WGP has very few leopards, thus making the disappearance of these extraordinary animals from the WGP something of a mystery.

NOTE: Notes on the hyena have been included here at the end of the section on the cats. This is because, though doglike in appearance, with legs and feet that are typical of the dog family, science has decided that the structure of the animal's skull and teeth, as well as certain other aspects of its anatomy, relegate it to the cat family.

THE PANDAS

THE CAT BEAR or RED PANDA, *Ailurus fulgens* (F. Cuvier). Taru names not available. Nepalese: *wah,* or *nigalva ponva.*

The Red Panda is found in the temperate forests of the Himalaya. Its range includes Nepal and Sikkim, and extends eastwards into Burma and southern China. As its distribution is described as being over 5000 feet, it is not likely that it will be found in the WGP and the author has never seen one there. However, as the possibility has never been explored, I will include it.

The animal is terrestrial, taking to trees to sleep or when alarmed or threatened. It is almost completely vegetarian in diet. Adults measure 24in, with a tail of about 16in. Coloration is a bright chestnut red. The tail is ringed, the face is white and it has a vertical red stripe from the eye to the nape.

A pair lived in captivity at the Royal Hotel in Katmandu in the 1960s. They were never quite tame, and their habit of biting people unexpectedly and refusing to become 'housetrained' made them unpopular pets. But like many Asian animals that are captured and sold as pets, they had probably been, initially at least, ill-treated by their captors.

THE DEER

THE SAMBAR, *Cervus unicolor* (Kerr). Taru: *Sambar*. Hindi: *Sambar*.

The Sambar is the largest of the Asian deer. (The second largest is the Kashmir Stag; this is not found in Nepal.) Adult males stand up to 5ft at the shoulder and weigh up to 700lbs. The animal is brown in color with a grayish tinge. The horns are massive, with a brow tine and a single fork at the summit of each beam. Their food is grass and leaves; Sambar are both grazers and browsers. They will also eat fruit when it is available.

They are nocturnal in their feeding, lying up in dense thickets during the daylight hours. They swim with ease; large rivers do not impose boundaries to their territories. Their principal enemy is the tiger and, of course, poachers. Leopards will rarely take one of the animals; their massive bulk deters the big cat. Their alarm call is a single but continuous, loud and distinctive bell-like peal. Their principal habitat in the WGP is mainly in the northern areas of the park, in the Bhabar region, close to the hills. They are seldom seen in the park itself.

THE SWAMP DEER or BARASINGH, *Cervus duvauceli* (Cuvier). Rana Taru: *burrasingh or gond*. Hindi: *barrasingh*.

The Swamp Deer is a big, coarse-coated animal, with males standing 54in at the shoulder. The general coloration is a

The Deer

yellowish brown; males are darker than females. The weight of an adult can be as much as 400lbs. They are principally grazers. Their horns are massive; they consist of a brow tine on the main stem and, at the top, from 10 to 14 points. In the WGP they live mainly in the central grasslands of the reserve. A few inhabit another small swamp area called Sundari Jal, north and a little west of Singpur. In the 1950s, when I first went into the WGP, large groups of the animals lived permanently in the Andaneha. In recent years, however, they seem to have abandoned these wetlands and moved out into the phantas; this may be because the vegetation there, mainly elephant grass, has thickened considerably and is now extremely dense, especially along its border with the grasslands.

In the grasslands they are subject to some poaching by Indian poachers from the south, across the Indo-Nepal border. The meat from the animals they kill is dried and sold in markets; apparently it is a popular food in the Indian market. For myself and my clients, in the days when we hunted the animals, we found it quite unpalatable, coarse, stringy and strong-tasting. Poaching of these deer is done with muzzle loaders, the limited range of which requires that the poacher must stalk to within thirty feet of his target. In the thick grass of the *phantas* this is not difficult. Poaching is usually done in the early evening when the poachers know that the park Game Scouts will have gone home for the day; a kill made at sunset will also allow the poacher the cover of darkness to cut up the carcass and get back with it over the border to India.

The WGP herd in 2005 comprised about 1500 animals. The alarm calls of the *barasingh* can be compared to the braying of a donkey; when several hundred call at once, the noise is considerable. When grazing—during which large groups will eat together, all facing in the same direction—they make a continuous mewing sound, which may be a form of family communication. The name *barasingh* means 'twelve-horned' and refers to the average number of tines the males carry. But some Tarus say that the name is actually *burra singh*, meaning 'big-horned'. The Swamp Deer is now an endangered species, and the WGP herd may well be the last herd of any substantial number left in Asia.

THE CHEETAL or SPOTTED DEER, *Axis axis* (Erxleben). Taru: *cheetal*. Hindi: *cheetal*.

Mature members of this species stand 36in at the shoulder and can weigh up to 190lbs. Their horn structure is similar to that of the Sambar, with a single brow tine and a forked, two-pointed top. Their coloration and the pattern of their hides—dark spots against a rufous fawn background—is designed by nature for camouflage, and in the dappled light of the Terai forests, which is their principal habitat, it could not be more perfect.

In the WGP they live in herds of up to eighty or more. They feed in the morning and afternoon, and will lie down in the shade during the midday hours. They are often found feeding with Rhesus Macaques and Langurs (monkeys); in the reserve they will venture far out into the open grasslands of the *phantas*, where they will sometimes graze in close proximity to Swamp Deer. A reddish-colored Swamp Deer, observed and photographed by me in the *phantas* in 1995, with a distinct set of Cheetal horns, suggests the possibility of (limited) hybridization between the species. The Cheetal is the most common of the deer of the WGP and is the principal food of both the tiger and the leopard. At this time they do not appear to be endangered.

THE HOG DEER, *Axis porcinus* (Zimmerman). Rana Taru: *parua*. Dangora Taru: *para*. Nepalese: *laguna*.

The Hog Deer is next down in size from the Cheetal. The height at the shoulder is 24in. The horns rise from extended bony pedicels and the beam supports a single brow tine and then rises to a single fork. Average horns measure 12–15in and the record horn is 24in. In coloration, the animal is a light brown; old males are darker. It has a slightly bowed back, sloping down, forwards, from the rump, and it runs with its head down; a bodily shape and practice that enables it to move swiftly through dense cover.

Hog deer are generally solitary, but in the WGP they have been observed in pairs and in small groups of up to ten. Their principal habitat in the WGP is the central grasslands, where they live in the shorter grass of the phantas. They are also found in some of the other phantas of the reserve, which provide them with the thick, short grass that is their desired cover. They are not found in thick, high grass—elephant grass—which they seem to avoid, or in the forests of the park.

They have excellent hearing—essential for the survival of animals living in dense cover—and an acute sense of smell. They feed in the early morning and late afternoon, lying down in cover during the heat of the day. They are very shy animals and run for cover at the approach of a vehicle; in places where there is human habitation, they may become nocturnal. The mating season is in the fall of the year and, with an eight-month gestation period, the young are born in the early summer. They are preyed upon by both tigers and leopards. The WGP has a healthy population of this small, pig-like deer, which, related as it is to the Cheetal, is known sometimes to interbreed with its larger cousin.

THE MUNTJAC or BARKING DEER, *Muntiacus muntjac* (Zimmermann).
Rana Taru: *kakara*. Dangora Taru: *gotra*. Nepalese: ratua. Hindi: *karkar*.

The Barking Deer is the smallest of the deer found in the WGP. Its bright, chestnut coloration blends well with the *sal* forest that is its principal habitat. Adult males stand a maximum of 30in at the shoulder and weigh about 50lbs. Horns of male animals, less the pedicels, seldom exceed 5in, with the pedicels usually measuring 3–4in. The pedicels extend down either side of the face, a peculiarity that at one time caused the animal to be known as the Ribfaced Deer.

An additional oddity with this animal is the large size of the upper canines of the males—something, like the 'wing' bones of the tiger. These may be described as vestigial but are still used by males in self defense. The horns comprise a short, stumpy, brow-tine and the beam is not forked. The horns, like those of other deer, are dropped yearly; the pedicels, however, are permanent fixtures. Females are hornless and the little animals live either alone, in pairs, or sometimes in small groups, browsing and grazing on grass, bushes and wild fruit.

In areas where there is minimal human presence, such as in the WGP, the Barking Deer is diurnal. Its name comes from its alarm call, a single but continuous, doglike bark. It calls when it sees anything that it considers dangerous, including humans. When the object of its alarm disappears from its sight, the calls cease.

NOTE: There are three other deer found on the Indian subcontinent. One is the KASHMIR STAG, a resident of Kashmir. Another is the CHEVROTAIN, or MOUSE DEER, a little creature that stands about ten inches at the shoulder and is found only in south India and Sri Lanka. The other is the MUSK DEER, the habitat of which is the high Himalaya. The known and established habitat of these three species precludes the possibility of them being found in the WGP.

THE ANTELOPES

THE NILGAI or BLUE BULL, *Boselaphus tragocamelus* (Pallas). Rana and Dangora Taru: *nilgai or nilgaia*. Nepalese: *nilgai*. Hindi: *nil, or nilgai*.

The WGP has a small population of these magnificent animals, the largest of the Asian antelope. Bulls stand up to fifty-six inches at the shoulder and their coloration is a bluish gray; their young, and females, are tawny. Males have short thick, hollow, cone-like horns which, unlike deer, are not shed annually. These are triangular at their base, shaping to conical at the top. The horn averages 8in. Both males and females have manes; males carry a short, thick, black tuft of hair on the throat.

The WGP *nilgai* prefer forest as habitat and in the reserve this means the sal forests. Until recently these forests were outside the reserve and were subject to heavy cattle grazing. As a result, in many places, the ground in the forest between the standing trees is almost completely bare of vegetation, making it unlikely habitat for the Nilgai. However, now that this land has been incorporated into the reserve, cattle-grazing has ceased and, within a monsoon or two, the forest should be naturally restored.

Two areas of forest seem to have permanent groups. One of these is the forests of the reserve's new eastern addition, east of the canal and south of Bhatpuri Lake. The other is the section of sal forest in the north-central area of the park, bordered on the west by the Singpur to Majgoan road, on the east by the Singpur to Malu Mela road and in the south by the Crosslands road (see map). The addition of new waterholes in this area, an area previously dry through the winter months, should serve to increase its Nilgai population.

THE BLACKBUCK or INDIAN ANTELOPE, *Antelope cervicapra* (Linnaeus). Rana and Dangora Taru: *mirga*. Nepalese: *krishnasagar*.

The Black Buck (also written Blackbuck) is a strikingly marked and graceful antelope. Males stand 32in at the shoulder and may weigh as much as 90lbs. The young of the Terai Black Buck are pale yellow in color. At the age of three they turn black. The animal is a creature of the open plains and will seldom venture into forest. It has very keen eyesight and uses this as its main instrument of defense, detecting danger at considerable distances and immediately taking evasive action with a run that begins with a series of giant leaps and then settles down to a steady gallop. They are grazers, living mainly on wild grasses, but they will also invade domestic crops. Horns of the males are spiraled and hollow; females may sometimes have small horns. The horns are not shed annually, like those of deer.

A fine herd of 45 animals lived in the *phantas* of the WGP until the early 1970s. Then, one by one, they fell victim to poaching; the skin of the males is highly prized as an ornamental rug and also for use in Hindu religious ceremonies. This was the only group in the WGP and, with their disappearance, the animal is no longer to be found in the reserve. (A second group of about forty animals lived in the vicinity of the Taru village of Kalkutta, east of the WGP. They too fell victim to poaching and are now all gone.)

The Antelopes

THE FOUR-HORNED ANTELOPE or CHOW-SINGHA, *Tetracerus quadricornis* (Blainville). Taru: *charsingh*. Hindi: *chowsingha, or chowka.*

The *chow-singha*, which means four horns, is a small and graceful little animal with two sets of horns, one set behind the other. The smaller horns are always in the front. Unlike other antelopes, the horns are not ringed but keeled in front. Females are hornless. Males stand 25in at the shoulder. Coloration is reddish brown above and white below. I was able to observe and identify two Four-horned Antelope in the WGP, twice, in the mid-1950s. This was in among the small winter pools of the otherwise semi-dry, scrubby bed of the Sarda River, which is the western boundary of the WGP; the pools provided a habitat that would be suitable to what may be, in this animal, a constant need for water. Since that time I have not seen any, nor have they been reported in the park.

THE CANINES

THE WOLF, *Canis lupus* (Linnaeus). Taru: *jungli koota*. Hindi: *hundar or hurar*.

The Indian wolf is mainly a creature of open country and as such may always have been scarce in the forests of the WGP. Taru villagers, however, insist that they see them in the grasslands from time to time. The animal stands 2ft–2ft 6in at the shoulder, and will weigh as much as 60lbs. Wolves are both nocturnal and diurnal; they may live in anything from small packs to single animals. Three to nine pups are born to a litter and their life duration, from domestic records, can be as much as 15 years. I have encountered the Indian wolf at 10,000 feet in the eastern Nepal Himalaya—the upper Arun Valley—but not in the WGP.

THE JACKAL, *Canus aureus* (Linnaeus). Rana Taru: *sera*. Dangora Taru: *giddar*. Hindi: *seall*.

Similar in appearance to the African jackal and the American coyote, the Asian jackal stands about 16in at the shoulder and weighs about 20lbs. The coloration is dark gray, washed with buff. The WGP jackals seem to live mainly in pairs, although pack assemblies have been seen from time to time in numbers of about a dozen. They are both nocturnal and diurnal. As well as being hunters of small animals, they are also excellent scavengers, using their keen sense of smell to home in on decaying carcasses from considerable distances. They are omnivorous and, in addition to flesh, will eat fruit, berries and seeds.

Their wild, long, drawn-out, eerie calling, the meaning of which is still not completely understood, is an integral part of the chorus of the jungle night. They are harmless to man, but, given the chance, will readily prey on domestic stock such as fowl, goats and sheep.

What else they will eat—their other food—is, I believe, deserving of an anecdote. In the 1940s, when I was a tea planter, I kept two young jackals as pets for a while. This was in north Bengal, an area where, during the rains, millions of insects were constantly on the move. In those days, with the war just over, we had not yet managed to get wire screen netting for our bungalow windows. At night, the summer heat—for we had of course no air conditioning—forced us to keep our windows open for air. The oil lamps we used at that time attracted thousands of insects, mostly moths and beetles, many of which, crashing into walls and furniture, usually finished up on the floor. This nightly buzzing, droning, whining and fluttering invasion quickly came to an end with the arrival of my two young jackals, for from the day they came to live with me, not a single moth or beetle (or spider, centipede or scorpion) lasted for more than a second or two after entering the house. Many of them were actually taken in the air, my two agile little friends leaping 3–4ft up to snap them up as they came flying in. From this I learned, at least, that insects form a large part of the diet of the jackal in the wild.

THE RED FOX, *Vulpes vulpes* (Linnaeus). Rana Taru: *seria*. Dangora Taru: *feowra*. Hindi: *lomri*.

The Red Fox measures a little more than 2ft in length, with a tail of an additional 18in. The weight of an adult male is about 12 lb. The animal is basically red in color, but this can vary according to season. They have been seen in the WGP, but are rare. They live in pairs; six or seven pups are produced in a single litter. Their principal food is rodents, but they are omnivorous and will also eat berries, seeds, some plants, fruit and the combs of wild bees. Again, if hungry, they will scavenge around villages. In cold weather they sleep with their large, silky-haired tails curled around their heads and faces. Their nocturnal call is an eerie single scream, oft repeated. The Taru people say that they will consort with a tiger, following him when he sets out to kill and then, after waiting for the big cat to eat, take their own share of the prey. In my opinion it is doubtful that any other animal will consort with a hunting tiger. But it is possible that this shy and secretive little canine might follow a tiger in the hope of a meal after the big cat had finished eating.

THE RED DOG, *Cuon alpinus* (Pallas). Rana and Dangora Taru: *ban mahola*. Hindi: *jungli koota or dhole*.

The Red Dog is also known as the Indian Wild Dog and the Dhole. Its basic overall color is red, though this can vary with the season. It stands about 18in at the shoulder and will weigh up to 40lbs. In the WGP, it has been seen in both the open grassland and the depths of the forest.

It lives by hunting and is diurnal in habit. Its prey is detected by scent and then pursued by sight. The pursuit is silent when in the open, but subject to yipping barks when the pack is in brush or forest; this may be a method of communication between pack members while in fast movement.

Its food is mainly deer. Once an animal is picked out as prey, and the pursuit begins, it is doomed. The chase may continue for miles if necessary, until the prey collapses or turns to stand at bay. When this happens, its pursuers close in, ripping, tearing and even starting to eat while the object of their pursuit is still alive. Usually the prey usually dies of shock.

The Canines

Nothing, it is said, can stand against the Red Dog. Tireless in pursuit and utterly ferocious in attack, they have been known to drive a leopard off its kill or even attack it and, in some cases, in spite of fatalities in the pack, kill the big cat. The Taru name, *ban mahola*, is very apt; the word *ban* means forest and the word *mahola* means king, giving the Red Dog what is probably a very deserving title ... king of the forest.

THE SWINE

THE INDIAN WILD BOAR, *Sus scrofa* (Linnaeus). Taru: *suir* or *sungur*. Nepalese: *baneel*. Hindi: *suir*.

Adult wild boar will stand 36in at the shoulder. The average weight of mature males of the species is 350lbs, but many larger animals have been recorded. The Indian record, for a specimen shot by a British hunter in Uttar Pradesh at the turn of the century (i.e. around 1900), is 745lbs. In the WGP the animals are generally smaller and adult males average 275–300lbs, females 20–30lbs less. The basic color of both males and females is black. The young are born with brown, horizontal stripes running along the flanks; this coloration fades and disappears with age. In the WGP I have noted more than a few adults with a light brown coloration; perhaps this suggests some interbreeding with domestic animals.

The animals are omnivorous and will eat just about anything, including the meat of rotting carcasses. They feed in the early morning and late afternoon. They are mainly diurnal, except where there is human presence, when they will revert to nocturnal feeding. They have a very keen sense of smell, but moderate eyesight and hearing. They are intelligent animals and their courage when challenged is legendary; big boar have been known to stand up to a tiger and even fight to the death.

For many years the WGP has had ample wild boar and it was possible to see single individuals or small sounders of the

The Swine

animals all the time. Then, around about 1995, they started dying out. Suddenly, all that one saw were very sick, slow-moving, very emaciated single animals, sometimes just standing in the forest with their heads down. I do not know what disease struck them, but something did, possibly a virus. Since then, however, they have come back and once again (2005) they can be found throughout the reserve.

Unless one has the ability to stalk them, which not very many people have, the best way to view wild boar in the WGP is from a vehicle. Sometimes, at the approach of a vehicle, they will simply bolt. At other times, if the vehicle stops and its occupants keep quiet and still, they may come within a few feet, the sound of the running engine seeming to be of no concern to them. They also have a peculiar habit when encountered by a vehicle and while feeding close to a jungle road. They hesitate for a few seconds, presumably to size up the situation and then bolt down the side of the road. Then, instead of cutting off into the forest, they cross the road at speed, immediately in front of the vehicle, and then disappear into cover. Why they do this I do not know, but I have seen it many times.

In the WGP there are always one or two sounders to be found in the northern end of the park, in the forest around Kumari Tal and in the Haria grasslands. Another place for viewing is the *phantas*, especially in the early morning and late evening, when they come out of what seems to be their desired habitat, the little islands of trees, to forage and dig for roots.

They are easily tamed if captured young, and make good house pets. I kept two in north Bengal in the 1940s. They were affectionate, playful and very clean animals, being almost completely odorless; also, as long as they could get out of the house whenever they wanted to, they were naturally housetrained. One night, after about six months of living with me, they went outside after dark and simply disappeared. Whether they were victims of a leopard, or a pack of jackals, or a roving hyena, I do not know. I never saw them again.

The White Grass Plains

Wild boar breed throughout the year and the period of gestation is about sixteen weeks. Litters average about six. When about to give birth, the sow builds a big igloo-shaped structure of grass and tree branches, and the young are born inside this. If one is on foot, it is advisable to stay away from these pig houses when they are occupied by pregnant sows.

THE PIGMY HOG, *Sus silvanius* (Hodgson). Taru: generally, *chota suir*. Nepalese: *sanu baneel*.

The Pigmy Hog is a diminutive member of the swine family, standing 10in at the shoulder and weighing, fully grown, about 15lbs. A shy and secretive animal, it is said to live in sounders of up to twenty animals. Very little seems to be known about its habits. However, it may be safe to assume that these are similar to those of its big brother, the wild boar.

In the 1960s I was commissioned by the Mayo Clinic to find and capture some specimens. A member of the Mayo family, Joe Mayo, joined me for a three-month search. We traveled the length of Nepal, west to east, by four-wheel-drive vehicle, with a three-man camp staff and fly-camp equipment. Our basic search method was to show villagers pictures of the little pigs in the hope of finding a group. In a village in far eastern Nepal we met a villager who had one as a pet. He told us that there were no more in his area and that he got his when his village dogs chased a group and scattered them, killing some. We bought the specimen from him for $2. However, it died before we could get it back to the U.S. The general feeling about the Pigmy Hog is that it may now be extinct in Nepal. None have been seen in the WGP for many years.

THE SAURIANS

There are three species of crocodile on the Indian subcontinent—the *mugger*, or Marsh Crocodile, the Estuarine Crocodile and the Gharial. Two of these, the *mugger* and the *gharial*, are found in the WGP. Crocodiles are very ancient animals, dating back one hundred and ninety million years. Their ability to survive so well is probably due to their needs being very minimal—basically flesh of any kind, in any state of decay—plus the fact that they live on the edge of two life zones, water and land, both of which supply these needs.

Sight, smell and hearing are very well developed in the crocodile, and all three senses are used in their hunt for food. Their usage also contributes strongly to their extraordinary ability to make an attack on an animal they have pinpointed at the edge of a river or lake. The codes for this firmly fixed in their brains, they will submerge to make their attack. The underwater approach, swift and silent, may be through moving currents of water, which, because of silt, debris or lack of light, will have minimal visibility. But when the saurian emerges for the attack, it will be at the precise place where the target was pinpointed.

Their teeth are shed and constantly replaced throughout their lives and they lay oval, hard-shelled eggs, which, for purposes of incubation, are buried in the sandy soil of riverbanks or in nests made of soil and vegetation. The nests are guarded by the mothers and it is inadvisable, especially with the *mugger*, to get between the female and the nest when walking a riverbank. The mother will react vigorously if she feels the young are threatened in any way, and the result can be dangerous.

Crocodiles are extremely agile in water, as well as which they can walk comfortably out of the water, with the body fully raised from the round. On land, if alarmed, or if attacking an animal, they are capable of great speed over a short distance, perhaps as much as 30 miles per hour.

Crocodiles are water-based animals, but at the same time spend much of every day basking on land at the water's edge. This is because of their need, as animals with a low metabolic rate and no sweat glands, to regulate their body temperatures. They do this with a judicious use of sun and shade using either, alternately, to regulate their body temperatures, nearly always lying with their mouths open, another method of heat control.

While the *gharial* is a fish-eater and, as such, not dangerous to man, both the Estuarine and the *mugger* will take human prey if they come across it, especially at night, making it dangerous after sundown to go into any water where they have habitat. In Nepal, the human fatality rate is low, native villagers being all too aware of the danger the *mugger* represents, especially after dark. But occasionally a man or a woman is taken, usually one foolish enough to attempt to cross a jungle river at night, or even to get too near to a riverbank. To the crocodile, with its small brain and its ability to catch and kill just about any land animal that ventures into the water, anything that moves, especially at night, means food. I know of only two incidents where Taru men lost their lives to a *mugger*, both were taken at night.

In the old days, whenever a croc was shot, it was the habit of hunters to open up the stomach and see what was in there. The amount of women and children's jewelry that was found gave both the *mugger* and the estuarine croc a reputation that they really did not deserve, for much of this—cheap glass bangles, bracelets and beads—was from human carcasses.

The author taking advantage of a little elevation

The author with a 12 ft python, caught and released for study

The author with a locally made brick

The White Grass Plains

Peter Byrne, aged 83 in 2007, still enjoying life in the WGP

A cluster of tiny, unknown, pin-head-sized insects on a tree

The Saurians

An unknown insect on a tree

A Common Cormorant
on the Chaundar River

The White Grass Plains

A Crow Pheasant, also known as the Coucal, a scavenger bird

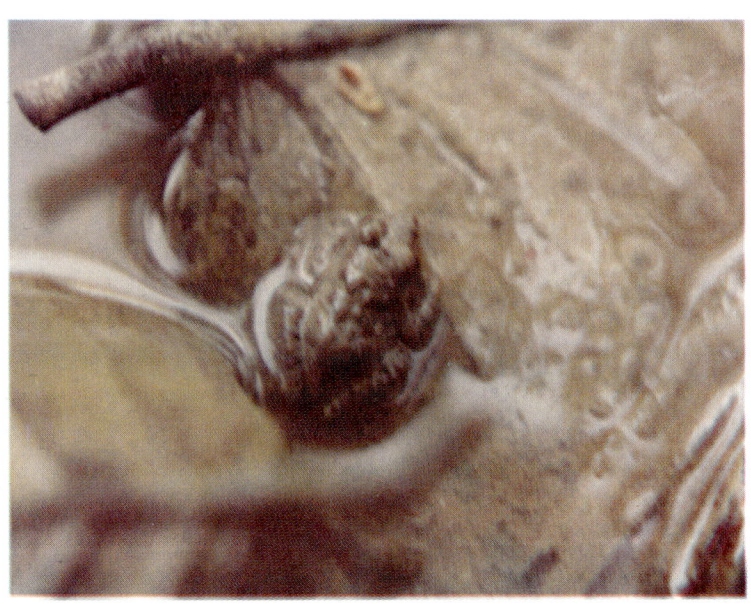

A frog in the Nilghai 11 waterhole

The Saurians

A good morning's sport on the Karnali River. PB, Thondup Sherpa

A wickedly sharp, hooked thorn frond known to the Taru as bh

A young mugger croc that took up residence near the author

A young rhino killed by poachers using a pit trap

Ancient river stone, burned by a thousand summer suns

Author's daughter, Rara at one of the huge stunted trees

The White Grass Plains

Bullock cart in the early morning mist

Cathy Griffin in the WGP

Cathy Griffin working (hauling water for cement mixing)

Eurasian kingfisher on the Bauni River

Chameleon, species unknown to author

Cheetal, or Axis deer in the WGP

Cormorants using dead trees as perches at Sal Gauni Tal

The White Grass Plains

Dung beetle cocoons. Expertly made by the female

Dung beetle cocoons. Expertly made by the female

Early morning in the WGP, with sunbeams like swords

The White Grass Plains

George Nathaniel Curzon, Viceroy of India, hunting tiger

Gharial, or long-nosed, fish-eating crcodiles on the Bhabai

These would most have been from poor villagers who, unable to afford the cost of firewood for cremation, disposed of by simply putting the bodies in the nearest river.

Also found in their stomachs from time to time were collections of medium to large-sized pebbles. These are intentionally swallowed by *muggers*, either as a contribution to digestion, or as ballast to assist in flotation and diving. A Karnali crocodile taken by a client of mine in the 1950s, and measuring 12ft in length, had 2.5lbs of pebbles in its stomach.

The big reptiles will hiss if they feel threatened, and from time to time will roar, a powerful, bellowing sound like that made by the domestic buffalo. Their normal vocal communication, however, seems to be confined to a series of grunts. Hatchlings in their eggs will also call if they are disturbed or threatened, a high-pitched distress call that will bring adults in the vicinity charging to the rescue.

The Karnali River gorge had a fine population of crocodiles at one time—fifty or so. On several occasions I enjoyed viewing them from a small plane, flying with the legendary pilot, Captain Emil Wick at 20 feet above the water and watching them leap out of the rocks on either side to splash mightily into the green waters of that beautiful river. Then, in the 1980s, the Japanese employees of the company that built the Karnali bridge started shooting them for sport; within a year they were all gone.

I would regard both the Estuarine crocodile and the *mugger* as endangered at this time.

THE MUGGER or MARSH CROCODILE, *Crocodylus palustris* (Lesson). Rana and Dangora Taru: *naka*. Hindi: *mugger*.

The Indian crocodile is also known as the *mugger*, or Marsh Crocodile. It is a heavily built, semi-aquatic, carnivorous animal, the habitat of which is preferably the dark, slow-moving waters of jungle rivers and pools. In the WGP the *mugger* is found principally in three areas. One area comprises the upper and lower reaches of the Bauni River. Another is the Andaneha. A third is the lake of Rani Tal, both in the lake itself and in the marshy areas on the lake's eastern and northern sides.

Adults run up to 15ft in length, with an average length of about 12ft. Mature males may weigh as much as 800lbs. Coloration in juveniles is a light brown, with black bands on the tail and body. Adults are a basic gray, with flashes of dark yellow and brown on the upper body, the belly gray to off-white.

The *mugger's* food when young is crustaceans, frogs, small fish, small animals, water birds and even large insects. But when mature, their food is carrion and, in addition, literally any living thing that they can find and overpower in the water or on land. This will include large fish, snakes (including python), otters, all of the deer, any of the cats (up to something as big as a leopard), wild boar and monkeys, particularly the latter.

Like most animals, monkeys, both the Rhesus and the Langur, need to drink at least once a day. The Langur is normally able to satisfy its need for water by finding it in the form of dew or raindrops captured in leaves or hollow places in tree trunks, high above the ground. But the Rhesus does not have this habit, and its need for water means that it must descend to the ground to seek it, at the bank of a river or pool. This habit and need makes them very vulnerable to the waiting *mugger*.

Probably, like many if not all animals, they seem to be oblivious to the dangers presented by the *mugger*. On hot days they will actually come to a river to forage on the branches of overhanging trees, inches above its surface. When they do this, their young, especially sub-adults of the *macaques*, will play and swim both in the water and even underwater, a risky habit in mugger territory that must in the long haul have serious consequences for the little animals.

Muggers live by hunting and scavenging. They are able to detect rotting carcasses at a considerable distance. Animals of all kinds that have died in the water—perhaps fallen in and drowned—form a major part of their diet. The carrion will include the remains of animals both wild and domestic, including, among the latter, cows, buffaloes, horses, donkeys, sheep, pigs, goats and dogs.

They hunt in the water at night, silently cruising their territories, submerged to where only their eyes and their nostrils, the latter conveniently placed in the tip of the nose, are above the surface of the water. Or they may lie in ambush, watching and listening for any animal entering their domain. Once the prey is detected, the saurian pinpoints the place and then moves, swiftly and silently, under the surface, to the attack. Arriving at the precise place where the prey was pinpointed, the croc may, if the prey can be seen, visually attack it. If the prey is not visible, perhaps having departed, then it will usually make a violent, biting lunge at where it was when it was pinpointed, hoping to catch it in its jaws.

When a hold is made on the prey, it is dragged into the water and submerged and drowned, the *mugger* holding on until all physical movement has ceased. It will then take the carcass to a chosen place to eat. If the body is small and thus subject to quick dismemberment, it may start to eat it at once. But if the prey is large, big-boned and difficult to physically tear apart, it will lodge it in the mud of an underwater bank, or thrust it into the roots of a submerged tree and leave it there to decompose. To protect the cache from other animals-mainly its own brethren-it will stay in the vicinity for several days, patiently waiting until the muscles and tissue of the carcass begin to disintegrate. Then when it determines that it is ready to eat, the croc will pull it out of its place of lodgment and, with a series of violent side-to-side movements with its neck and jaws, break it up and eat it, swallowing the rotting flesh in large chunks. The reason for this method of feeding—waiting for natural decomposition to soften its food and then swallowing it in large, unmasticated pieces—is that the *mugger* has no cutting teeth in its jaws, teeth that would allow it to chop up its food into easy-to-swallow portions. Its teeth are designed to bite and hold only; they are structured, in other words, for the killing process of firmly seizing an animal and holding it underwater until it drowns.

While most of the *mugger's* hunting is carried out in water, it will also hunt on land at night. In the WGP I have observed and recognized signs of the reptile's stealthy, nocturnal passage—smeared mud on leaves and grass caused by movement through the undergrowth—sometimes as far as 300 yards from the nearest water. (Something to keep in mind if one is considering walking around at night in the vicinity of jungle rivers or pools!) The mugger can walk well on land, lifting its body completely off the ground and traveling on all four feet. In the water the feet are not used for propulsion; this is done by the perfectly adapted and powerfully muscled tail.

At this time (2007) the WGP seems to have a fairly well-balanced population of these ancient and fascinating reptiles, with probably between seventy-five and a hundred as its resident population. On the upper and lower Bauni River, their habit of basking in the sun enables them to be viewed and photographed after a quiet approach. Those at Rani Tal can be observed and photographed from a small boat or, in places where the mud is not too deep, from elephant back. The Great Swamp also has crocodiles and possibly some very big ones. But the Andaneha is mostly impenetrable, its dense grass and deep, cold, muddy water masking its secrets well.

THE GHARIAL or LONG-SNOUTED CROCODILE,
Gavialus gangeticus (Gmelin, 1789). Rana and Dangora Taru: *gharial*. Nepalese: *chimpta, or gohi*. Hindi: *gharial*.

The *gharial*, also known as the *gavial*, is a large, fish-eating saurian found throughout the Terai of Nepal. At one time there was a small population living in the lake of Rani Tal, in the WGP. When Taru villagers—then living in the park, but since relocated—accidentally drained the lake by digging a canal from it to their rice fields, the Rani Tal gharials disappeared. In 2003 I observed a single species in the lake. Plans are presently being discussed with the Department of National Parks and Wildlife to relocate additional members of the species to the WGP from central Nepal, where breeding programs have increased their numbers.

The gharial is one of the largest of the Asian saurians, with adult males measuring up to 15ft. It has long, narrow jaws, with interlocking, knife-edged teeth, especially designed for seizing fish in the water, which it does with fast, lateral, snatching movements. It has 25 to 26 identical teeth in the upper jaw and 25 to 26 in the lower. The first three teeth of the upper jaw fit perfectly into recesses in the lower. At the end of the snout, adult males have a large, bulbous growth, which looks like a native, earthen pot known in Hindi as a *goila or gara*. From this comes the animal's name, *gharial*.

Coloration of the big reptile is a dark to brownish olive, with yellowish-white under parts. The young are a pale brown; they have five broken transverse bands on the body and nine on the tail.

The young make a peculiar groaning sound when disturbed, and adults will bellow like a buffalo when agitated. Males when breeding hiss like a crocodile does when it is disturbed.

The big reptile's rear feet are webbed for assisted underwater locomotion; its primary propellant is its tail. Unlike the *mugger*, it is not adapted to movement on land, where it is only capable of slow, clumsy movements, so it seldom strays far from water. Juveniles will eat frogs, small fish, lizards and crustaceans. Adults live mainly on fish, seizing them in their agile jaws and then manipulating their bodies so that they can be swallowed headfirst. If hungry, however, they will also eat turtles, water birds and small mammals.

THE APES, MONKEYS AND LEMURS

In Asia there are two species of ape. One is the Orang Utan of Sumatra. The other is the Hoolock, or White-browed Gibbon, which has habitat in the forests of Assam, east of the Brahmaputra River—fondly known to us in the days of the Raj as the Burrumpooter—and ranging all the way from there to the Salween River in Burma. Both animals are true apes—tailless primates like their cousins the gorillas, chimpanzees and bonobos of Africa.

In the same great landmass, including the Indian subcontinent and in some cases the Terai of Nepal, there are ten species of monkey and two species of the quaint little creatures that are of the same genus, the lemurs. The lemurs are the Slow Loris and the Slender Loris. The monkeys are, firstly, the macaques; the Rhesus Macaque, the Assamese Macaque, the Bonnet Macaque, the Liontailed Macaque, the Stumptailed Macaque and the Pigtailed Macaque. And, secondly, the langurs, including the Common Langur—also known as the Hanuman Monkey—the Golden Langur (discovered and classified by a friend of tea-planting days in Assam, E. P. Gee), the Capped Langur, or Leaf Monkey and the Nilgiri Langur.

Of the loris family, the Slender has known habitat only in south India and Sri Lanka, thus can hardly be considered as a possible resident of the WGP. The same applies to the Slow Loris, which is only found in Assam, Tipperah and the Chittagong forests.

Of the langurs, only one species, the Common, is liable to be found in the WGP. Of the macaques, two, the Rhesus and the Assamese, can be found in the WGP, the former in fairly large numbers.

THE RHESUS MACAQUE, *Macaca mulatta* (Zimmermann) Rana and Dangora Taru: *bandar or lal bander*. Hindi: *bandar*.

The Rhesus Macaque is one of the most common monkeys of the subcontinent, with multitudes of them living in forests, grassland, villages, towns and cities. Adults measure 24in head to rump, and weigh about 20lbs. Females are smaller, about 18in long, and weigh about 12lbs. In the WGP they live mainly in the forest and are seldom seen in the grasslands. Constantly needing water, they prefer forest close to a river or pool. Arboreal little mammals, they spend a lot of time feeding on the ground, something that makes them vulnerable to predators, particularly the leopard, which seems to be their principal enemy.

They are herbivores, but are said to eat flesh if it is readily available, such as carrion. Their principal food is ground plants, all kinds of weeds, flowers and shoots, but they will also eat berries, fruits and insects, such as spiders and beetles. They swim well, both on the surface and underwater, something that makes them vulnerable to both mugger croc and python. They seem to mate throughout the year—indeed, vigorously, it would seem, whenever they can. Though their numbers were greatly depleted in recent years with their capture and export for medicinal use—mainly in connection with the polio vaccine program—the cessation of this practice has allowed them to regain their vast numbers and as of now they are definitely not endangered. They do not make good pets, tending to be mischievous, short-tempered and given to biting their hosts. Of this latter, the author speaks from experience!

The Rhesus, like all monkeys, have very keen eyesight and when they are in the trees can always be depended upon to spot an approaching predator and give warning to all the jungle folk. Unlike the Langur, at the sight of a leopard the Rhesus will seldom drop to the ground and try to outrun it, not allowing their fear to blind them to the fact that they are relatively safe as long as they remain in the trees.

Rhesus troops may number anything from twenty to fifty, or more. In appearance they seem to be simply a collection of monkeys that have got together for protection. But in reality the groups are close-knit, each and every one related to another in some way; every single member of the troop has its own special identity, a fact brought home to me by an amusing if perhaps tragic incident.

Some years ago I acquired a young Rhesus macaque as a pet, a male about five months old. It lived in my safari camp and at first behaved quite well. But it soon showed its true colors and within a month had turned into an ill-behaved little menace. Its behavior included raiding the kitchen, biting the cook when he tried to prevent it from stealing food, getting into tents, stealing all kinds of articles of clothing and generally making an irritating nuisance of itself. It reached the point where my high-paying safari clients were complaining. So I decided to return him to the jungle, and to do this by finding a troop of his little brothers and sisters and simply handing him over.

Early one morning I drove out into the forest and found a troop of Rhesus, walked up to them, dropped the camp monkey on the ground and walked away. The young Rhesus took one look at its brown brethren in the trees above, gave a scream of horror and bolted back to the car. I tried again a second time and the same thing happened, my little companion bolting in terror and this time reaching the car before me. The third time I tried, several male members of the chosen troop actually dropped from the trees and chased the unwanted youngster for his life.

After this third try, while I was sitting on the road in my car, wondering what to do, a passing group of Tarus stopped to ask me if I had a problem and needed some help. Yes, I said, and explained what I was trying to do. Whereupon they said that they would be happy to take the little monkey off my hands, and that it looked like a nice pet. I promptly seized on the offer, the camp pet was duly handed over and that was that, problem solved, and a new home found for the mischievous little menace. Or so it seemed. But a week later I was told an interesting story by a Taru village friend, about an enjoyable, curried, monkey-meat dinner to which he and his wife had been invited by a cousin. Oddly, the date of the dinner was the same as that on which the camp pet changed ownership.

One learns from incidents like this-my monkey rehabilitation failure- in this case the obvious fact that Rhesus monkeys are highly family-oriented and also strongly territorial, unhesitatingly closing ranks against an outsider, even one of their own species.

At night Rhesus macaques roost in trees off the ground, the young with their mothers, males in small groups, and old males sometimes alone. Finding suitable perches for the night, and determining who gets the best ones, produces a lot of grumbling argument from the adults and whimpering complaints from the young.

Rhesus are often seen foraging on public highways. What takes them there is food, usually grains of rice, or pieces of sugarcane, dropped from passing trucks or carts. When encountered like this by an approaching vehicle, they show unusual common sense and never hesitate to leave the pavement well in time, staying off it until the vehicle has passed. In Nepal, the larger primate, who is their cousin, supposedly the more intelligent one, could learn a lesson or two from this.

In regard to the leopard being their principal enemy, I had an unusual experience some years ago. Driving past a troop of them sitting in a Strangler fig tree in the forest, a wool, leopard-patterned rug, lying on a seat back and visible to them in the open car, suddenly put them into a high state of alarm, with males growling and snarling, females screaming, young panicking in all directions. When I stopped the car they immediately surrounded it, though without coming lower than 20ft above the ground, gnashing their teeth and screaming their rage and fear at what they obviously thought was their mortal enemy, Mr. Spots.

THE ASSAMESE MACAQUE, *Macaca assamensis* (McClelland). Rana and Dangora Taru: *bhandar*. Hindi: *bhandar*.

The Assamese macaques were fairly common when I was a tea planter in the Dooars district of north Bengal in the 1940s, and hunted and fished the splendid jungles that lay between the two great Terai rivers of that area, the Teesta and the Toorsa. Their general habitat is described as ranging from Mussoorie, in northwest India, all the way east to the great delta of the Bramaputra that is called the Sundarban. But the boundaries of habitat are often flexible. So it was that we saw them often, distinguishable from the Rhesus by the absence of the dark red rump and the red coloring of the loins.

The Assamese is about the same size as the Rhesus, 24in, but a little heavier, as much as 20lbs. In social patterns it is also similar, surviving in medium to large troops and spending much time in the trees. Like the Rhesus, its principal enemy is the leopard and, foolishly, like the Langur—but unlike the Rhesus—it will sometimes drop to the ground in panic at the sight of a big cat and make the fatal mistake of trying to outrun it.

For my book about man-eating tigers and leopards, GENTLEMAN HUNTER, a study was done of the comparative running speeds of tigers and leopards. It was determined that at full speed, flat out so to speak, the leopard can run, albeit for a short distance, at 52.8 miles per hour, which means that it can cover 100 yards in three seconds. It is very doubtful that the Assamese macaque, though nimble and fast in movement, can equal this incredible velocity.

The food of this agile little Assamese simian is fruit and insects, the latter including beetles, grubs, worms, caterpillars and grasshoppers. These are caught with great dexterity by hand and then popped quickly into the mouth. They will also raid domestic crops, and can do a lot of damage in just a few minutes in a villagers' vegetable patch. Whether or not they eat meat is not known, just as their breeding habits in the wild are still something of mystery.

I personally have not seen any in the WGP, but this does not mean they are not there. Like many another unknown animal possibly living in the sylvan forests of the WGP, determination of the fact is a challenge for future researchers.

THE COMMON LANGUR or HANUMAN MONKEY, *Presbytis entellus* (Dufresne). Rana and Dangora Taru: *Langur.* Hindi: *Langur or hanuman.*

This animal is the big, common, black-faced monkey of India. Mature animals of the WGP have a body size of 26–30in, with a tail of the same length. Their weight will range from 35–45lbs. Coloration is a uniform gray and they have black faces. However, there are variations in color between the different races, one of these being the brown variety found in the upper reaches of the Tula Beri River area and identified by me there in 1980.

Langurs of peninsular and south India are a little smaller and lighter. Those of the northern groups, like the so-called Himalayan Langur, are bigger and heavier, with a very dense coat and a thickly furred tail. I identified a troop of fifteen of them one morning, squatting on the bare branches of a Chir pine, at Rara Lake, 13,000 feet above sea level, their off-white coats glistening with the ice particles of an early morning frost. Contrary to opinion, the Himalayan Langur is not a separate species but just one of the races, or variations, of the common species.

The Langur is more consistently arboreal than the macaque, preferring to stay in the trees as much as possible. Much of their food—flowers, buds and leaves—is obtainable above ground; they satisfy their need for water, again high in the trees, by drinking raindrops or dew that has gathered in cupped leaves or hollow places in trunks.

Langurs commence feeding soon after dawn, rest during the hottest part of the day, and feed again in the evening. They will happily consort with macaques, separating from the other species at dusk to go their separate ways to their sleeping roosts. In their roosting trees they sleep high up and as far out on the thin ends of branches as they can, a common safeguard of the species against a prowling, tree-climbing predator.

Langurs live in groups of 20–80. When feeding, they move from tree to tree in great crashing leaps, often accompanied by whooping cries. The noise they make in this movement, plus their habit of tearing off the bark of dead trees in search of grubs, is only matched by the foraging and feeding of a group of elephants.

The foraging range of a troop varies from 1–5 square miles and is determined by the amount of food that the area makes available to them. The breeding season in the WGP seems to be November and December. The gestation period is about 180 days and a noticeable birthing window appears to be April and May. Mothers carry their young with them until they are mature, making their traditional great, leaping bounds with the young holding on to the fur of their stomachs or their backs.

The leopard is the inveterate enemy of the Langur; many fall victim to its silent and deadly hunting. While high in the treetops, they are of course quite safe, and if the cat is spotted, a male member of the group will immediately make the traditional, deep-throated, grunting alarm call—a single grunt, a double grunt and then a triple grunt—something that gets the immediate attention of the troop and temporarily freezes all movement. But the need for food will sometimes find them foraging on the ground, where a hungry leopard, taking advantage of every inch of cover to remain unseen, may be able to get close for the lightning rush and the single bite that is all that is needed for a catch and a kill.

Mr. Spots also gets his Langur meat dinner in another and somewhat unique way. Homing in on the sounds of a feeding troop, he makes a silent and unseen approach, to get as close as possible. When he is within about 20 yards of the tree in which the troop is feeding, he steps into the open and announces his presence with a deep-throated, guttural roar. This produces instant alarm among the feeding simians, some of which, in wild panic, will foolishly drop to the ground and try to make a run to safety. The big cat is, of course, much faster over a short distance and the object of its attack is usually caught and killed within seconds.

Why langurs continue to do this, and why they have not learned how deadly the results can be when they leave the high terraces of their aerial domain with their deadly enemy, a leopard, in sight, is something of a mystery. Panic—sheer terror at the sight of the big cat—may simply override their common sense and cause them to act as they do. It is interesting to note that the Nilgiri Langur, whose habitat is in the Nilgiri Hills in south India, does the same thing when approached by native hunters with packs of dogs, foolishly leaping from their safe, arboreal retreats and leaping to the ground in panic; in this case they are chased and quickly run down by the dogs, with similar fatal results.

THE SNAKES

No scientific studies have ever been done on the snakes of the WGP, so the following listings and descriptions are based on my field observations and experience. These listings include some snakes which, because they have known distribution that includes the Terai, may well be found in the WGP.

Here, for the purpose of clarification, the snakes that are known to be in the WGP and the others that verified distribution indicates may be there, I have divided into two categories, poisonous and non-poisonous.

THE NON-POISONOUS SNAKES

THE PYTHON, *Python molurus* (Linnaeus). Rana Taru: *Chitti saap, burra saap*. Hindi: *azgar*.

The greatest of the non-poisonous snakes of the WGP is the python. In this case the species is the Indian Python, also sometimes called the Asiatic Rock Python.

The python of the WGP are typical of the species, that is to say big, slow-moving reptiles, with bodies rounded in the center and tapering towards the head and the tail. The head is flattened and leads into a long snout. General coloration is a yellowish gray, and the creature's pattern includes a series of roughly quadrate patches that run dorsally and are outlined in black. The pattern includes a large lance-shaped mark, with a

The Snakes

light center, on the back of the head. The eyes are small and the iris is flecked with gold. A peculiarity of the reptile is a set of curved, eagle-like, sharp-pointed talons set in the skin at the rear of the animal's body, on either side of the anal orifice. These are believed to be vestigial remnants of limbs from a time when a direct ancestor of the animal had legs.

Python are oviparous, the females laying clutches of eggs that may number as many as 100. These large clutches may have to do with the rate of attrition caused by predators, such as the monitor lizards. The nest may be a shallow depression in the ground or a hole in the bank of a ravine. After laying her eggs, the female may stay with them for up to two months until they hatch. During this time she will not hunt or eat.

Python eggs are about the size of a small domestic chicken egg and are much the same color—a flat, slightly off-white. However, their contents—which include the embryo and the yolk on which it feeds until it emerges from the shell—are enclosed in a tough, protective, semi-elastic skin and, were it not for a unique device naturally supplied to the embryonic python, getting out of it might pose a problem. This device is a shell-cutting tooth, called an egg-tooth. It is a small, temporary, sharp-edged tooth that grows on the outer edge of the upper jaw; the young python uses this to literally hack its way through the walls of the shell to the outer world. Soon after use, the little tooth drops off. Python young may be as long as 28in when they hatch. Their growth is rapid, to a length of 78in within a year and up to 108in in 24 months.

The WGP pythons grow to a considerable size, with some adults reaching 20ft. Specimens of 14ft are not uncommon and I have manually captured and released big males of up to 18ft. A 17ft specimen was found dead on the south bank of the old Chaundar River drainage, in the winter of 1998–1999, possibly killed by a tiger, and I personally believe that much larger specimens, in excess of 20ft, may be found in the as yet unexplored inner reaches of the Andaneha.

Though generally harmless to man, there have been some instances of small children being taken and eaten, one of these a young girl in the Indian province of Uttar Pradesh in 2006. Adults of up to about 12ft in length can be captured by hand, and I have done this several times for purposes of study and photography, the reptile then being released. Capturing one longer than 12ft requires the assistance of two extra men to hold the reptile while it is being photographed and measured. The most important part of capture and release is being able to hold the animal's head. The coils, though powerful, can be resisted without great difficulty, but the snake will bite if it can and the danger from a bite lies in the possibility of decayed animal tissue in its teeth, which could cause septicemia.

The python's food, just like that of many predators, includes anything that it can overpower and kill and it will include birds—especially water birds that swim, which are easily taken from below the surface—rats, small mammals including monkeys, jackals, porcupines, the smaller deer and the young of all deer. Two dead pythons that I discovered in the WGP, both killed and partially eaten by leopards, had medium-sized mammals in their stomachs—in one, a civet cat, in the other, a jackal. The prey is swallowed whole, usually head first, its passage down the snake's throat being assisted by copious amounts of saliva.

This great snake is a strong swimmer and quite at home in the water, where it can remain submerged for up to 30 minutes. It will use water as cover in which to lie and wait for its prey, remaining partially submerged, with just the tip of its snout showing. It will also lie in ambush alongside game trails. It takes its prey by seizing it in its strong jaws and then, using the powerful coils of its body, kills it by constriction that induces suffocation.

The WGP pythons may spend much of their nocturnal hours in water, either hunting or resting. But the daylight hours are mostly spent basking in the sun in some warm place. This habit of lying in sunlight has to do with the fact that, unlike mammals, the python—and indeed all snakes—does not have the physical ability to control its internal body temperature. From this comes their reputation of being cold-blooded, which is not quite true. They are actually warm-blooded, but, unlike mammals, need to work to retain a healthy physical temperature. So nature has endowed them with the intellect to do this by moving from place to place, using sunlight and shade as necessary to keep their bodies within the required temperature ranges. This vital requirement, to balance their internal metabolism, is why the WGP python can often be found, in the daytime, lying out in the sun on the banks of rivers and pools. Unlike certain other snakes, which because of climatic changes are forced to hibernate, the WGP pythons stay active throughout the year.

The principal enemies of this unique snake are poachers—who kill them for their marketable skins, crocodiles and hunter-predators, like leopards, hyenas, jackals and wild dogs. A fully-grown specimen will be able to fend off attacks by jackals and hyenas, and possible even leopards. But sub-adults are vulnerable. Tigers on the whole do not seem to regard them as worthwhile prey.

In the WGP the principal habitat of the python is the upper reaches of the Bauni River, waterholes such as the Hidden Springs waterhole, the Nilgai waterholes, the Hatti Pokri waterhole, the wetlands that surround the lake of Rani Tal and of course the Andaneha.

The other non-poisonous snakes that have general Indo-Nepal habitat including the Nepal Terai, and thus may possibly be found in the WGP, include two other constrictors—John's Earth Boa and Russell's Earth Boa. With them, in the same non-poisonous category, though not as constrictors, are the Common Worm or Blind Snake, Diard's Worm or Blind Snake, the Trinket Snake, the Copper Head Snake, the Dhaman or Common Rat Snake, the Fasciolated Rat Snake or Banded

Racer, Gray's Rat Snake, also known as the Glossy-bellied Racer, the Royal or Diadem Snake, the Common Kukri Snake, the Common Indian Bronzeback or Tree Snake, the Painted Bronzeback, the Golden Tree or Flying Snake, the Common Wolf Snake, Shaw's Wolf Snake, the Checkered Keelback, the Buffstriped Keelback, the Olivaceous Keelback, the Green Keelback, the Condanarous Sand Snake, the Indian Gamma or Cat Snake, the Common Green Whip Snake, Schneider's Smooth Water Snake and the Indian Egg-Eating Snake.

Of these non-poisonous snakes, in addition to the python, I have positively identified two species in the WGP. These are the Fasciolated Rat Snake, also known as the Banded Racer, and the Flying Snake.

The Banded Racer is an olive-brown snake with a yellowish-white belly and large, gold-ringed eyes. Adults, which grow to about 45in, have minimal markings, but the young are strikingly ornamented with black and white crossbars and green bellies. The food of this fast-moving snake is small mammals, mostly rodents and amphibians.

The Flying Snake, also called the Golden Tree Snake, is one of the most beautifully ornamented and colored of the snakes. The reptile is slender, with a pear-shaped head. It is generally pale gold in color with black crossbars on its body. The head is black, with yellow crossbars. Distinctive to its markings are a series of dark orange, flowerlike imprints running down the back. Interestingly, these beautiful markings are very similar to those seen on one of the larger fishes found in the WGP's Bauni River, a fish classified as *Channa marulius*, known to Nepalese as the *bhaura*, and to the Taru people as the *ghate*. (See THE FISHES.)

The Flying Snake is arboreal and diurnal; it feeds mainly on lizards. As well as moving with ease through the branches of trees, it can effortlessly climb perpendicular trunks. Like the Flying Squirrel, it is not a true flier, but a glider. Traveling from tree to tree, its launches itself into the air from a branch, or the trunk, from a coiled position and with a springing motion. Immediately it is airborne, it applies a muscular action to hollow its belly into an elongated, cupped shape that in effect forms an air-gathering wing and assists flight. In flight it is said to keep the body rigid. Flight is used as a form of locomotion, with single glides carrying the little reptile distances of up to perhaps 50 yards.

NOTE: One other species of python, the RETICULATED PYTHON, is common to the Indian subcontinent. As far as is known, it is not found in the Terai of Nepal, its habitat being recorded as eastern Assam, the Nicobar Islands, Bangladesh, the Malay Archipelago and the Philippines. In size, the Reticulated Python is longer then the Indian Python and is generally recognized as the longest snake in the world. There is a record of one of thirty-two feet. At the same time, it is not the biggest or heaviest of the world's snakes, this distinction being given to the Anaconda, a giant snake found in South America, east of the Andes. In the northern reaches of its range, the Anaconda grows as long as twenty-nine feet. But it is its bulk rather than its length that makes it the world record holder for size. One nineteen-foot female measured thirty-six inches in circumference and weighed two hundred and thirty-five pounds. Proportionately, a thirty-foot Anaconda could weigh five hundred pounds.

THE POISONOUS SNAKES

The poisonous snakes that may have habitat in the WGP include the Common Indian Krait, the Banded Krait, MacClelland's Coral Snake, the Indian Cobra, the Monocellate Cobra, the Black Cobra, the King Cobra or Hamadryad, and the Russell's Viper.

Of the poisonous snakes listed here, the author has identified three in the WGP. These are the Black Cobra, the Russell's Viper and the Banded Krait.

The White Grass Plains

The Black Cobra is normally found in the extreme northwest of the Indian subcontinent. Accompanied by a Taru tracker, Narain, from the village of Jillmillia, I identified one on the east bank of the Bauni River, about one mile north of the Bauni bridge, in the winter of 2002. Its length was approximately 6ft, its coloration black. It was initially detected, by both of us, because of the light reflecting off the top of its shiny head. We spotted it from a distance of 20ft, lying coiled in the roots of a large tree. On seeing us approaching, it immediately rose from the ground, flaring its hood. However, when we remained quite still, it gradually sank down, then turned and disappeared quickly into the root system of the tree. The Black Cobra is described as generally being non-aggressive but quite the opposite if disturbed and provoked. It is both nocturnal and diurnal, and its bite can be fatal to man.

The only Russell's Viper that I have found and identified was discovered on the south bank of the Hidden Springs waterhole. My Taru work crew, cleaning out the waterhole, mistakenly identified the snake— which was covered with gray ash from a grass fire—as a young python. To calm them and allow the work to continue—for Tarus are always nervous around snakes and seldom identify them individually—I picked up the reptile by hand and released it into the spring. However, when the water washed the ash off its skin, and its pattern appeared, it was apparent that it was a Russell's Viper, a very dangerous snake, and one that should never be handled manually.

My encounter with the Banded Krait took place on the construction site of the new conservation and research center which I am building in an area called Bagh Phanta—the Plain of the Tigers—just outside the southeastern boundary of the WGP. (See notes and full description of this at the end of the book.) The date was 08 November 2006 and it was early evening. One of the construction masons, Mr. Bheem Singh, noticed something moving along the base of the brickwork at the back of the new building. Recognizing it as a snake, he immediately sent two men to call me. Armed with a powerful flashlight, I went to the site. The snake was a Banded Krait—the coloration, black and yellow rings that went all the way around the body, being unmistakable. Using a short length of bamboo, the reptile was very carefully picked up and placed in a plastic bucket with a lid. The following morning I released it on the far side of the boundary river (to the relief of the workforce!) and, in the bright winter morning's sun, positively identified it and photographed it. I was unable to find any records of the effect of a bite by this snake on a human being. However, THE BOOK OF INDIAN REPTILES, by J. C. Daniel, makes a note that attracts the attention of the 185-pound author, which is that a domestic buffalo—an adult member of the species will weigh 2000lbs—died twenty minutes after being bitten.

Also identified in the western Terai, in 1999, not in the WGP but in the lower reaches of the Rapti River of the Dang Valley, was the Common Krait, a potentially hazardous snake. One was found hibernating in a hole in a sandbank by my daughter, Rara, while she was constructing a dirt stairway from the river up to the camp kitchen. On being disturbed, it struck fiercely at a stick that I was holding. However, on being released into the river, it quickly swam away.

THE LIZARDS

THE COMMON INDIAN MONITOR, *Varanus Bengalensis* (Schneider). Rana Taru: *baragwoi*. Dangora Taru: *ghoti*.

Adult monitors of this species are gray above, with some black spots, yellowish below, with scattered black flashes, and with a single dark line on either side of the head. The reptile lives in holes in the ground or in hollow trees, or hollow tree limbs. It is an agile climber and is comfortable at considerable heights above the ground. The largest recorded in the subcontinent was just under 6ft.

In the WGP, this monitor is found throughout the reserve, wherever there is suitable habitat and lair availability, such as in the banks of deep, dry *nullahs*, or large, old trees with hollowed out trunks, or hollow limbs. One lived in the broken end of a hollow tree limb high above the kitchen of one of my Bauni River camps, from where it would sit and peer down at my cook making dinner. It was there for many years, only leaving to find a new abode when the aged tree fell.

The animal is diurnal, though prone to be more active in the early morning and late evening. In some areas this could be because of the presence of man. Its enemies are poachers—for the reptile skin trade—jackals, hyenas, leopards and wild dogs. As the reptile spends time in water and will swim on both the surface and underwater, the *mugger* croc can be added to its list of enemies.

When alarmed by the presence of a predator, the monitor will at first 'freeze' and thus try to remain undetected. If the predator then attacks it, or threatens attack, it will run off at considerable speed, its intention being to get to its burrow, or tree hideout, as quickly as possible. On entering its bolthole, the animal will inflate itself to prevent being pulled out by the predator. Once inflated, it becomes firmly lodged and only a powerful predator, such as a leopard, might be able to pull it out.

This monitor hunts on the ground, traveling slowly with its tongue flicking in and out, watching for its prey. It hunts visually and also possibly, like some snakes, by scent detection—i.e. the collection of scent particles—through its tongue. Like most predators, the animal will eat whatever it can overpower and kill. Its known food includes rats, mice, squirrels, birds and their eggs, fish, crabs, fresh-water prawns, the eggs of many reptiles and the eggs of turtles. It is also known to take roosting bats, climbing high into trees for this purpose.

In the breeding season, males have declared territories and fight with other males for possession of females. After laying her eggs, the female monitor buries them in a pit that she then covers up, using her nose for this purpose. She may also then construct false pits, close by, as a decoy against egg-eating predators. Egg clutches vary in number from 10–25 and, generally speaking, the young are born in the first weeks of the monsoon.

THE YELLOW MONITOR, *Varanus flavescens* (Gray).

The habitat distribution of the Yellow Monitor is listed as being the Gangetic Plain from northeastern India to Bengal and Bihar. This would allow it to be included as a resident of the Terai—which abuts on to the eastern end of West Bengal—and as such be a possible resident of the WGP. In habits this reptile is similar to the Common Monitor, though its coloration is different, the animal being a yellowish brown with, during the monsoon, wide red banding, markings which fade and become less visible in the dry season. It is mainly crepuscular in habit, using the dull light of early morning and late evening for its hunting forays.

THE WATER MONITOR, *Varanus salvator* (Laurenti).

The range of this large lizard includes Bengal, Orissa, eastern India and Bangladesh. This expansive habitat may include the Terai and, possibly, the WGP.

This monitor is the largest of the monitors of the subcontinent, with males recorded at close to 7ft. It differs in habit from the other monitors in that its desired habitat is water, both inland fresh water and coastal salt water. Being almost entirely totally aquatic,, its food will be whatever it can find in its watery habitat; one, captured and dissected, had forty frogs in its stomach. It will, however, also eat the eggs of birds and, when it can, domestic poultry. It breeds at the beginning of the monsoon and females lay their eggs in dirt holes in banks, in hollow trees and in termite mounds.

NOTE: One other species of monitor is found in the Indian subcontinent. This is the DESERT MONITOR. As it is a creature of dry, sandy, desert country, with a habitat listed as northwest India and Pakistan, it is probably not to be found in the WGP. But, like the snakes, no studies have been carried out in the WGP on the monitors, as a result of which it is not positively known what other monitor species may exist in the reserve.

THE GECKOS.

The Gecko is a member of the lizard family and in the subcontinent can be found from the plains up to 15,000 feet in the Himalaya. The species may be terrestrial or arboreal. They are possessed of extraordinary climbing abilities and can traverse a flat ceiling, upside down, as easily as they can climb a smooth, vertical wall. They are principally insectivorous, but some are herbivorous. Certain of the larger species are carnivorous and will eat whatever they can overpower and kill, including other geckos and some of the lesser snakes. In turn, of course, they are vulnerable to the killing and eating attentions of all of the smaller predators of the forests.

Geckos that may be found in the WGP include the Northern House Gecko, some of which I saw in 1965 in an old government guesthouse, which has since collapsed, at Singpur. Other species include the Bark Gecko, Brook's Gecko, the Southern House Gecko, the Termite Hill Gecko, the Tucktoo, the Banded Gecko, the Frilled House Gecko, the Eastern House Gecko and the Banded Scaled Gecko.

THE SKINKS.

Skinks are small lizards that mainly feed on insects. The largest of the species found in the Indian subcontinent grows to a maximum of 18in. Their bodies are covered with smooth scales and the development of their limbs ranges from fully functional to vestigial to none. They are mainly terrestrial, spending their lives under the debris of the forest floor. Some species, however, are semi-arboreal. Among the species that may be found in the WGP are the Common or Brahminy Skink, the Little Skink and the Snake Skink.

THE GLASS SNAKES or GLASS LIZARDS.

Glass Snakes, or Glass Lizards, are distinguished from true snakes by the presence of eyelids, true snakes having only a membrane behind which the eye moves. Glass snakes, or lizards, are terrestrial, making their habitat under rocks and fallen trees; their food is mainly worms and insects. If attacked by a predator, the tail, like that of the gecko, can be dislocated and dropped. They breed in the rainy season and hibernate in the winter. One species, the Burmese Glass snake, has been found both in Shillong, in Assam, and in Simla, in north India, which suggests that the intervening country of the Terai might contain some specimens. Because of this, the family is included as a possibility for the unstudied forests of the WGP.

THE AGAMIDS.

The Agamids are Old World lizards and in appearance look like the iguanas of the Americas. They are separated from all other lizards by the structure of their teeth, which include canines, incisors and molars. They have habitat throughout the Indian subcontinent and elevations of up to 15,000 feet in the Himalaya. Some members of the genus are gliders, like the Golden Snake and the Flying Squirrel. They are quadrupeds, but if chased by a dangerous predator may become temporarily bipedal, racing away at speed, upright on their two hind legs. Some are insectivorous, some herbivorous, some carnivorous. A few members of the family are ovo-viviparous, but the majority lay soft-shelled eggs which are buried in soil for incubation. Some have spines on their bodies, and in the mating season the males of several species are brilliantly colored.

Among the agamids that may possibly be found in the WGP are the Common Garden or Bloodsucker Lizard, the Forest Calotes, the Eastern Green or Jerdon's Calotes, the Fan-Throated Lizard, the Kashmir Agama, the Short-Tailed Agama, the Blue-Throated Lizard and some of the Japalura lizards, some of which are listed as having habitat in the western Himalaya.

THE LACERTIDS.

There are not many species of the family Lacertidae in the Indian subcontinent. This is a lizard with certain physical developments that separate it from other families. These include well-developed limbs—appendages that allow for great speed of movement on the ground—the presence of symmetrical shields on the head, and a notched tongue. The two species that do find habitat in India are known to have broad distribution; this is why they are included as possibles for the WGP. The two in question are Leschenault's Cabrita and Jerdon's Snake-Eye.

THE CHAMELEONS.

Chameleons are arboreal, diurnal lizards with extendable tongues, separately moveable eyes and a toe structure of opposed digits similar to those found in some birds. Their tails are prehensile and they have the ability to change color, something that makes them unique in the animal world. They are mainly insectivorous, but their food may include small amphibians, such as frogs. They hunt with their tongues, approaching within striking distance of their prey, focusing their attention on it and then striking it and seizing it in the viscid, club-shaped tip of the extendable tongue.

The capture strike is very fast and can be repeated almost instantly. Females lay eggs, which are then buried in the ground for incubation; the clutch can contain about thirty eggs. The incubation period in the wild does not seem to have been precisely determined, but is recorded as being up to nine months.

The single species for which the WGP may provide habitat is the Indian Chameleon, *Chamaeleon zeylanicus* (Laurenti), a moderately sized lizard with a maximum length of about 15in. Its basic color is green; its markings include black and yellow bands and spots. Like other chameleons, it has the ability to change color, but this may be limited to just green and yellow. Its body is covered with scales. Its eyes are large and, with the exception of a small aperture for the pupil, are covered with a scaled lid; they are also capable of independent movement and, from their unique position on the head, binocular vision.

Its hands, at the extension of its frontal limbs, have two opposed sets of digits, one set pointed away from the body, the other aligned towards the body. In the foot the formation of the digits is reversed.

The animal is diurnal and arboreal, slow-moving and deliberate and, with its particular coloration, well camouflaged by the green tracery in which it lives. Its food is mainly insects, large and small, but very small frogs will also be taken as well as the young of small rodents, such as mice.

The female descends to the ground when she is ready to lay her eggs. She will use her forelegs to dig a hole for these, then climb down into the hole and spend six or eight hours in it laying her eggs. When she has completed this, laying a batch of about thirty eggs, she will emerge and, using her forelegs to move dirt and her rear limbs to pack it, seal up the hole. The incubation period for the eggs varies from 3–9 months.

THE TURTLES AND TORTOISES

THE LAND TORTOISES.

The land tortoises of Asia live within thick, strongly built carapaces, or shells, and have heads and necks that are fully retractable. They are all grouped with a single genus, the *Testudinidae*. They are all herbivorous and oviparous, laying hard-shelled eggs from which their young are born. All are of moderate size and within a general shell size range of about 10in. Their ancestors, however, were probably much larger; the Siwalik Hills of India have produced fossil remains of a giant tortoise with a shell length of 7ft 6in.

Species which may be found in the WGP include the Starred Tortoise (which ranges through peninsular India all the way to Pakistan) and the East Asian Tortoise, which is recorded for Nepal. Other species found in the Indian peninsula, but at this time not listed for the Nepal Terai, include the Travancore Tortoise and the Eastern Hill Tortoise, the latter being the largest of the species in the subcontinent. One other species of the Asian land tortoises is found in Baluchistan; this is the Afghan Tortoise.

THE FRESHWATER TORTOISES.

Freshwater tortoises are also known as terrapins and in general appearance they look very much like land tortoises. They are mainly herbivorous, though some omnivorous species are recorded, the food of which may include the droppings of other animals. Young are produced from hard-shelled eggs, which are laid in small batches. Their basic habitat is in water, though some species are semi-terrestrial. Unlike the land tortoises, and as a means of locomotion in water, the digits of these mainly aquatic animals will be from partially to fully webbed.

Species which may possibly be found in the WGP include the Indian Pond Terrapin, the Chapant or Smith's Terrapin, the Dhoor or Dhongoka Terrapin, the Sail Terrapin, the Brahminy Terrapin and the Spotted Black Terrapin.

Other species found in the subcontinent, though not listed as having habitat in the Nepal Terai, include the Deccan Sawback Terrapin, the Khasi Hills Terrapin, the Eastern Hills Terrapin, the Batagur Terrapin and the Kerala Forest Terrapin, a small freshwater tortoise discovered in 1911.

THE FRESHWATER TURTLES.

Freshwater turtles, also known as mud turtles, have flattened shells covered with a soft skin. Their limbs have three claws and their heads and necks are fully retractable. They are fully aquatic, spending all their time in water and, with the exception of two species only found south of 20 degrees N. latitude, are common throughout the subcontinent.

Species which may be found in the WGP include the Indian Mud or Flap-Shell Turtle, of which there are two races, the Indo-Gangetic Mud Turtle and the Peninsular Mud Turtle. Of these, the Indo-Gangetic Mud Turtle is a WGP 'possible' in that its distribution includes the Indo-Gangetic Plain that abuts on to the southern Nepal Terai. The other race is less likely, its habitat apparently being confined to areas south of the Ganges and Sri Lanka. Other species that may have WGP distribution are the Chitra Turtle, the Ganges Softshell Turtle and the Deccan Softshell Turtle.

The Turtles and Tortoises

One other turtle is found in the subcontinent. This is the Peacock Softshell. It is not recorded for the Nepal Terai, its distribution apparently being confined to the lower reaches of the Ganges and Bramaputra rivers.

NOTE: The other turtles with distribution related to the Indian subcontinent are the marine turtles of the coastal waters and the islands of the Indian Ocean. These include the Green Turtle, the Olive Ridley Turtle, the Hawksbill Turtle and the Leathery Turtle. They have not been included as 'possibles' for the WGP, for obvious reasons.

THE HARES AND RABBITS

There are a number of species of hares in the subcontinent and they include the Cape Hare, common to Kashmir and the North West Frontier Provinces; the Arabian Hare, of Baluchistan; the Wooly Hare, with habitat in Ladak, Sikkim and Nepal; the Hispid Hare, which ranges through the Indo-Nepal Terai from Uttar Pradesh eastwards to the Dooars (of north Bengal) and Assam; the Blacknaped Hare of south India; the Desert Hare of India's dry zones, including Rajasthan, the southwest Punjab, Kutch and Kathiawar; the Rufoustailed Hare, which lives from the Himalaya south to India's Godavari River; and the Mouse Hare, a diminutive little animal, 6–8in in length, that has its home in the high Himalaya at altitudes of up to 14,000 feet.

There are no true rabbits in the Indo-Nepal region, though the Hispid Hare closely resembles and relates to the rabbit and in Assam is actually known as the Assam Rabbit. Of these eight species, two, the Rufoustailed and the Hispid, may be found in the WGP.

THE RUFOUSTAILED HARE, *Lepus negricollis ruficaudatus* (Geoffroy). Rana Taru: *carghose*. Dangora Taru: *nama*. Nepalese: *carrio*. Hindi: *cargosh*.

This little animal measures, head and body, from 17–19in in length and weighs 4–5lbs. Their coloration includes a rufous brown coat with black fur on the back and face. The breast and the legs are rufous-colored, and the chin and upper throat are white.

In the WGP, hares are mainly found in the central grassland, though they will also enter the forest. Their food seems to be mainly grass. They are both nocturnal and diurnal. During the day, when not feeding, they will lie up in a patch of grass, making a comfortable little nest with their paws. Lying in one of these little homemade hollows, they are hard to detect, which is well, for they have many enemies. These include leopards, wild dogs, jackals, foxes, mongoose, wild cats and even village pariah dogs.

When discovered by a dangerous predator, their single defense is flight, and from the nest they take off at great speed in an effort to outdistance a pursuer. At the end of several short bursts of flight they may stop to take stock of the situation, sitting up high and looking around; then, if necessary, they will run again. At times they will take refuge in a porcupine hole or burrow. The little animal can run at great speed, but I have seen a jackal catch one at night. The chase, briefly illuminated by car headlights, was brief; it ended, in the darkness, in a despairing scream. The Rufoustailed produces one or two young at a time, but little seems to be known about their breeding habits.

THE HISPID HARE, *Caprolagus hispidus* (Pearson). Taru and Nepalese names: the same as for the Rufoustailed Hare.

This hare species is so named because of its rough and bristly fur. It is about the same size as the Rufoustailed hare, but with a much shorter tail, a bare one inch, including its terminal hair. Due to an intermingling of different colored hairs—black, white and brown—the animal generally appears as dark brown. Very little is known about this quaint little animal, though villagers say that, like a rabbit, it will dig a burrow, or use the burrow of

The White Grass Plains

another animal. It seems to be generally regarded as rare, the last known report being many years ago, from the north Indian Uttar Pradesh district of Kheri, which, interestingly, lies adjacent to the Nepal border, a few miles south and east of the WGP.

THE WEASELS

The weasel family, the Mustelidae, includes Badgers, Ferret Badgers, Ratels, Martens, Otters and the weasel itself, of which there are several forms. The Indian subcontinent, including Nepal, contains an unusual variety of this genus. The list includes the Common Otter, the Smooth Indian Otter, the Clawless Otter, the Beech or Stone Marten, two species of Yellow-throated Marten—the Himalayan and the Nilgiri—the Himalayan Weasel, the Marbled Polecat, two species of Ferret Badger—Chinese and Burmese—the Hog Badger, the Ermine or Stoat, the Pale Weasel, the Yellow-bellied Weasel, the Striped-backed Weasel and the Ratel, or Honey Badger. Of this splendid assembly, eight are found, or, because of their known distribution, could be found, in the WGP. They are as follows:

THE COMMON OTTER, *Lutra lutra* (Linnaeus). Rana and Dangora Taru: *ooud*. Hindi: *ooud, or ooud bilao*.

Adults measure 2ft–2ft 8in, with a tail of 1ft 6in. The animas are predators and hunt either singly, in pairs or in packs. Their principal food is fish of all kinds, but they will also eat leaves and water plants, frogs, crustaceans, crabs, small rodents and even waterfowl, which may be attacked and taken from below water level. When a large fish is caught it is usually brought ashore to eat, with all members of a hunting party joining in.

In the WGP I have seen them in the Bauni River, the lower Chaundar River and the Hidden Springs waterhole. A group of otters seen by the author at Rara Lake, in the high Himalaya, in 1983, were probably Common Otters.

One of their methods of catching fish is for groups of six or eight to swim in line abreast, with single members leaving the moving line to dive in search of prey and then quickly surfacing, a fish in the mouth, to rejoin the line. Lairs are found at the water's edge, in the roots of large trees or in reed beds. They are profusely by the animal's droppings and this easy to find.. This otter is primarily nocturnal, but in places where they are undisturbed, such as the WGP, they will hunt in the early evening and through to the late morning. The gestation period of this species is about two months, and the young stay with their parents until fully grown. When I lived in India during the Raj, with colonials who liked to keep pets, among the favorites were otters; they were easy to tame and followed their owners around with the affection of dogs.

THE SMOOTH INDIAN OTTER, *Lutra perspicillata* (I. Geoffroy). Hindi: *oud*.

This otter is close in size to the Common Otter, with a body weight of about 20lbs. It is found from the Himalaya all the way to South India. Though designed for life in the water, if fish are not plentiful or if water sources dry up, the Smooth Otter will hunt in forest and scrub and even travel long distances overland in search of food. It will even hunt in salt water, and has been recorded at sea considerable distances from land.

THE CLAWLESS OTTER, *Aonyx cinerea* (Illiger). Taru names unknown.

The name of this species describes it well. Unlike other otters, the animal has only rudimentary claws which are dominated by the toe pads. Its size is 18–22in, with a tail of 12in. Its color is dark brown above and paler below. Adult animals weigh about 12lbs.

THE YELLOW-THROATED MARTEN, *Martes flavigula* (Boddaert).

The size of this beautiful animal is 18–24in, with a tail of about 16in. Coloration of the dorsal fur is deep brown, black and yellow; the throat is yellow, with dark bands marking the nape, and the forequarters are russet. The distribution of this species is mainly in the belt of Himalayan forest between 4000 and 9000 feet, but they can also be found in tropical forests right down into the Terai. This would allow for the possibility of habitat in the WGP.

This marten lives alone and is both diurnal and nocturnal, and hunts in trees and on the ground. In the trees their food is squirrels and birds, bird eggs and their young. On the ground they hunt small rodents, like rats and mice, but also take birds as big as pheasants. If their normal food is not available, they will eat carrion, snakes, lizards, insects, fruit and even nectar from flowers, including the big red blossoms of the *simul* or silk cotton tree. Apart from this, very little is known about the animals, including their breeding habits.

THE CHINESE FERRET-BADGER, *Melogale moschata* (Gray) and THE BURMESE FERRET-BADGER *Melogale pesonata* (I. Geoffroy).

Both of these species are found on the subcontinent, their range including from Nepal eastwards to Assam and Burma, their preferred habitat being both forest and grassland. Both species measure, head and body, about 1ft 6in, in addition to which they have a 9in tail. Likewise, both species are similar in coloration, with fur that varies from deep purplish gray to brown. The tips of the hairs are bleached, giving their coats a somewhat silvery tone. The facial markings, cheeks, nuchal stripes and underparts are yellow to off-white, and an off-white stripe runs from the top of the head, traversing the back all the way to the tail.

The animals are a mixture of both weasel and badger, from which comes the name. They have pointed snouts, which they use to probe for food, and long non-retractable claws designed for digging. Their resemblance to the weasel, rather than the badger, can be seen in their whiskers, their large ears, their longer limbs and tail.

They live and hunt alone and are nocturnal, lying up during the day in burrows of their own making and hunting only after the sun goes down. Most of their hunting appears to be on the ground, but it is believed that they also hunt in the trees; their long limbs and the striated pads of their feet suggest an inbuilt ability to climb. They are omnivorous animals, their food including small mammals, birds, fruit and insects of all kinds, including cockroaches.

THE HOG BADGER, *Arctonyx colaris* (F. Cuvier). Hindi: *bala sur.* Taru names unknown.

Adults measure, head and body, up to 28in, and have tails as long as 7in. Its usual distribution is in the eastern Himalaya and Assam, but I have seen one in the WGP, at night, in 1965.

The Hog Badger looks more like small bear with a long nose than a badger, the latter an animal with which I am familiar from a youth spent in Ireland. It has short thick legs and small rounded ears. In color, it is a mixture of white, buff and black, with a pale throat and dark stripe on the cheek. Overall, the animal has a dull, off-white appearance. It is omnivorous and nocturnal. It apparently has poor sight and so depends upon scent for its hunting. A very secretive animal, almost nothing is known about its diet, the only record of which is from captive animals—one of which ate fruit and vegetables, another of which enjoyed the meat of birds, mammals and reptiles. Like the true badger, of which there are none in the subcontinent, the animal is a burrower.

THE RATEL or HONEY BADGER, *Mellivora capensis* (Schreber). Taru names unknown. Hindi: *bejoo or bajra*.

The distribution of this animal is from the Himalayas to Cape Cormorin. Adults, with their tails, measure 2ft 6in in length and weigh about 20lbs. Their color of this small bear-like animal is basically gray with the underparts of the body black. The animal's shelter is a hole in the ground. It is a carnivore with a diet that includes mammals, birds, reptiles and insects. It is not a true carnivore, however, like members of the cat family, for it will also dine on fruit and honey when hungry. The animal is very courageous and, like its cousin, the African ratel, will not hesitate to attack a man if cornered or threatened. Because of its habit of leaping off the ground (for a biting, clawing attack in self defense) at roughly the height of a man's crotch, the African Ratel is usually given a wide berth by wary villagers. Whether the Indian Ratel also practices this scary habit is unknown.

THE INSECTIVORES

Insectivores are small insect-eating mammals, and the genus includes tree shrews, moles, hedgehogs and ground shrews. Moles find their food under the ground. Hedgehogs and ground shrews hunt and eat on the surface of the ground, and are joined there by tree shrews which, though their name suggests otherwise, are also terrestrial, taking to the trees only to escape the threat of danger. The list for the subcontinent includes the Indian Tree Shrew, the Malay Tree Shrew, the Longeared Hedgehog, the Pale Hedgehog, the Eastern Mole, the Indian Shorttailed Mole, the Whitetailed Mole, and the Grey Musk Shrew. Of these seven species, and because of their recorded distribution, three may be found in the WGP. These are as follows:

THE MALAY TREE SHREW, *Tupaia glis* (Diard). Taru names unknown.

The Malay Tree Shrew, with known habitat in Burma and Assam and into the eastern Himalaya, could be found in the WGP. Adults measure 7–8in, with a tail of about 9in. In appearance, the little animal is like a cross between a shrew and a squirrel. Its long nose makes it squirrel-like, and the remainder of its body, with its rounded ears and long tail, also contributes to this appearance. Its feet are also similar to those of a squirrel, with naked soles, long toes and sharp, curved and pointed claws that that allow for nimble climbing when needed. The coloration is a russet brown above with lighter underparts.

The Insectivores

Their main food is insects, but they will also eat fruit and possibly meat. They drink water and will bathe in small pools. They are easily tamed and, entering a village house, soon became an accepted member of the family, climbing on beds and tables to eat whatever they can find.

THE EASTERN MOLE, *Talpa Micrura* (Hodgson). Rana and Dangora Taru: *chechundar*. Hindi: *chechundar*.

The Eastern Mole is a tiny animal, measuring about 4in in length and with a rudimentary tail. Its coloration is a velvety black. In appearance it is cylindrical in shape, with a neck so thick and short that it looks like an extension of the body. The tail is very short and is often concealed under the hair of the rump. The forepaws are equipped with large claws especially designed for digging. The eyes are tiny and the fur is so thick that no soil sticks to it, when it is burrowing underground.

Its food is earthworms and insect larvae. It makes its home in a burrow dug into the roots of a tree, with extending tunnels to other tree systems, some of them as much as 50 yards in length. Found from the hill ranges of Assam to the central Himalaya, this little creature with its subterranean habitat could be found in the WGP.

THE GREY MUSK SHREW, *Suncus murinus* (Linnaeus). Rana and Dangora Taru: *chechundar*. Hindi: *chechundar*.

This is the shrew that in Europe we erroneously call the Musk Rat. But it is a true shrew, with a long pointed nose, depressed ears and teeth that clearly distinguish it from the rat family. Its head and body measure about 6in and it has a tail of 2in; its coat color is a pale gray tipped with brown. The animal has a gland on either side of its body that gives out a strong musk-like smell; hence the English name.

The little rodent's food is insects, including cockroaches, making it a useful and inoffensive creature in domestic surroundings. It is also intolerant of rats and will chase them out of a house. But sadly, its rat-like appearance and unattractive musky odor lead to its being killed indiscriminately, and whenever encountered. The animals breed while still in the sub-adult stage; two or three young are produced at a time. When giving birth, the females lie up in a nest of straw and dead leaves. The young quickly learn to go with their mothers on hunting sorties, following in a line behind, each tiny creature holding on with its teeth to the end of the tail of the one in front.

THE PANGOLINS

THE INDIAN PANGOLIN, *Manis crassicaudata* (Gray) and THE CHINESE PANGOLIN, *Manis pentadactyla* (Linnaeus).

The pangolin is a toothless, scaly, ant-eating creature that looks as though it has stepped out of a prehistoric world. One species, the Indian, has been seen by the author in the grasslands and forests of the WGP. (On two occasions I have been watched by the odd little creature, standing up on its hind legs like a kangaroo.) The second species, the Chinese, having distribution from south China to Nepal, may also be an inhabitant.

The two species differ in size and in certain other bodily features, but have the same feeding and other habits. The first, the Indian, measures 2–2.5ft in length, with a tail of 18in, and has 11–13 rows of scales around its body. The second, the Chinese, measures 19–23in in length, has a 13–15 inch tail and a body encircled by 15–18 rows of scales.

What makes the pangolin different from other animals is its body armor, which consists of rows of flattened scales that envelop its head, limbs, body and sides. The scales overlap and its underparts have a fine coating of strong, bristle-like hairs.

The food of this strange little creature is ants and termites, to capture which it uses its long, protrusible and glutinous tongue. Choosing an anthill or termite mound, the pangolin thrusts its tongue into the interior and then draws it out quickly with its food, the insects it eats, sticking to its tongue. These are promptly licked off and swallowed. With the ants and termites come their eggs, of course, and it is believed that the pangolin prefers these to actual insect bodies. The lower end of the animal's stomach usually contains a small quantity of pebbles. These, like the stones found in the stomachs of crocs, are probably an aid to digestion.

The pangolin is terrestrial. But they have been seen in trees, high off the ground, probably in search of Red Tree Ants, the big, football-sized nests of which are not uncommon in the WGP. Climbing, it uses all four feet, like a bear. Also, when aloft, it uses its prehensile tail for balance. It is the only animal in the subcontinent with a tail like this—one that can be used to grip and hold.

It is probably not as rare as is believed; being nocturnal, it is seldom seen. It digs its own burrows, in which it lies up during the day, its head comfortably pillowed between its forelegs, and its scaly tail, like battle armor, curled over and completely covering its whole body.

For its size, the pangolin is a powerfully built animal. Its forefeet are especially designed for digging and, when it detects a termite mound, or an anthill, which it does by scent, it digs into it with great energy, hurling the soil out between its rear legs. When threatened, if it feels that it is perhaps cornered and that flight is not the wisest choice for survival, it will curl up into a ball and lie still. When it does this, it is almost impossible to uncurl, defying the attempts of a man of average physical ability to unwind it, and displaying amazing strength for such a small animal.

THE MONGOOSES

Southeast Asia is home to six species of mongoose, an animal the origin of which is believed to have been Africa. The species are the Brown, the Common, the Crab-eating, the Small Indian, the Ruddy and the Striped-neck. Of these six sets of animal, three, the Common, the Small Indian and the Crab-eating, are found in the WGP. Distribution of the remainder, which is mainly central to south India, pretty much precludes the possibility of habitat in the WGP. (See Note.)

Mongooses were originally classed with civets. Then studies showed them to be a different family, with many aspects of their anatomy that made them quite different from civet cats. Mongooses, for instance, can live as herbivores but prefer meat. Civets, on the other hand are almost pure herbivores.

Mongooses are predators, not lacking courage in attack, and they will not hesitate to try and kill animals larger than themselves. Their method of attack is direct, fast and ferocious. Only with some of the larger poisonous snakes, like the cobras, will they use their extreme agility to parry and feint, waiting for the opportunity of a killing bite. Their principal food is insects, including spiders and scorpions, and, in addition, small creatures like lizards, crabs, frogs and rodents. The habitat of some of the species is restricted by terrain and food; they mostly occupy hill forests. But two of them, the Common and the Small Indian, have in time found themselves able to survive in all kinds of climatic conditions, from the torrid plains of India to 7000 feet in the Himalaya.

THE COMMON MONGOOSE, *Herpestes edwardsi* (Geoffroy). Rana Taru: *neura*. Dangora Taru: *sapt neuri*.

This sleek, ferret-like little predator measures 36in in length, of which half is its tail. The tail is tipped with white or red, but never (like the Ruddy) with black. The weight of an average male is about 3lbs; females weigh much less. Coloration is a yellowish-gray. Its range is the whole of India, from the Himalaya to Cape Cormorin and even beyond, to Sri Lanka. In its hunting it is both nocturnal and diurnal, and for habitat it will live in almost any kind of cover, from forest to grassland. Food of the Common, in addition to that listed above as being general to the other species, includes carrion, rats, centipedes, snails, birds eggs and snakes, at the killing of which they are adept. When available, domestic fowls, including ducks, chickens and pigeons, are included in their diet.

The Common breeds throughout the year, the female producing up to three litters within twelve months. The gestation period is about two months. The Common make good pets and, in days gone by, many of my tea planter friends kept one in their houses, which the friendly and active little animals kept clean of rats, mice and other vermin.

THE SMALL INDIAN MONGOOSE, *Herpestes auropunctatus* (Hodgson).

This mongoose is smaller than the Common, measuring 18–20in. It has a shorter tail and soft, olive-brown, gold-flecked fur. The animal is diurnal in habit and lives in burrows that it digs itself. It is a shy creature and spends a lot of time in cover. Its presence, however, can be detected by the worn trails that it makes by using the same pathways, day after day. Its diet is similar to that of the Common, but includes wasps. The gestation period is about 49 days. Its longevity is unknown, but can be judged to some extent by that of one who lived in captivity for eight and half years.

The Mongooses

THE CRAB-EATING MONGOOSE, *Herpestes urva* (Hodgson). This crab-eating mongoose is a big, strongly-built animal, 18–21in in length, with a tail of 10in and a weight of 4–5lbs. Its long, coarse fur is a dark gray in color, but with light tips on the hair ends which brighten the general tone. Distinctive to the animal is a white bar running from the angle of the mouth, back across each side of the neck, to the shoulders.

It makes its lair in holes in the ground. Its diet, as its name suggests, is crabs, but in addition it will eat fishes, frogs, mollusks and snails. It is completely at home in the water and spends much of its time hunting for food along the banks of streams and in shallows. One way in which it gets its prey is by feeling under rocks and river stones with its forepaws and seizing whatever it can find. A means of defense, if threatened or cornered, is to eject a powerful stream of noxious-smelling fluid out of its anus, using its large anal glands. In captivity, one lived for ten years.

NOTE: Here and there throughout this guide the reader will note my fairly frequent reference to the fact that the WGP is still very much unexplored, with little or no research to date on many of its natural treasures. So, when I see that the habitat for an animal is listed as being in the general area, say, of the lower Himalaya, or simply north India, I am inclined to include it, but always with a note describing it only as a WGP possibility. However, when the known habitat of the animal in question is given as a totally different area, such as the Nilgiri Hills, or Assam, it is not included. Which is why, for the mongooses, I did not include the Ruddy Mongoose, the known habitat of which is listed as the forested areas of central and southern India, the distance between the Terai and central India being in the area of 900–1000 miles. This makes the possibility of the Ruddy being found in the WGP very unlikely, except for the fact that in the fall of 2006 I twice identified a mongoose with a black-tipped tail, which is what the Ruddy has in its scientific description, and what distinguishes it from the Common.

THE RODENTS

The rodent family of Southeast Asia includes squirrels, rats, mice and porcupines, all of them basically herbivorous. Most are small animals, not very strong, yet through the ages they have managed to hold their own against a myriad of enemies. What has enabled them to do this is their secretiveness, their wariness, their cunning and their quite incredible fecundity, the latter a vital aspect of their survival, for they form the principal diet of many of the smaller predators. With more than a thousand known species, they comprise the largest single group of mammals on our planet. Their habitat is on the ground, under the ground, above the ground in trees, or in water. And in spite of legions of natural enemies, including man, they live and thrive in every country in the world, from sea level up to 18,000 feet in the Himalaya.

In Southeast Asia a large number of species exist. The list includes the Indian Giant Squirrel, the Grizzled Giant Squirrel and the Malayan Giant Squirrel; the Himalayan squirrels, which include the Orangebellied Himalayan Squirrel and the Hoarybellied Himalayan Squirrel; the striped squirrels, which include the Fivestriped Palm Squirrel, the Threestriped Palm Squirrel, the Dusky Striped Squirrel and the Himalayan Striped Squirrel. Two species of marmot: the Himalayan Marmot and the Longtailed Marmot. Two species of gerbille: the Indian Gerbille and the Indian Desert Gerbille. Ten species of the rat family: the Indian Mole-Rat, the Shorttailed Bandicoot, the Metad or Softfurred Field Rat, the Whitetailed Wood Rat, the

Giant silk cotton tree north of the WGP

The White Grass Plains

Heron known as a Paddy bird, for its frequent foraging

Hundreds of prints at the Nilghai Waterhole 11

The Rodents

Hunting days, 1954, in the WGP, before I turned to conservation

In the pre-dawn hunting hours, a leopard crosses the road

The White Grass Plains

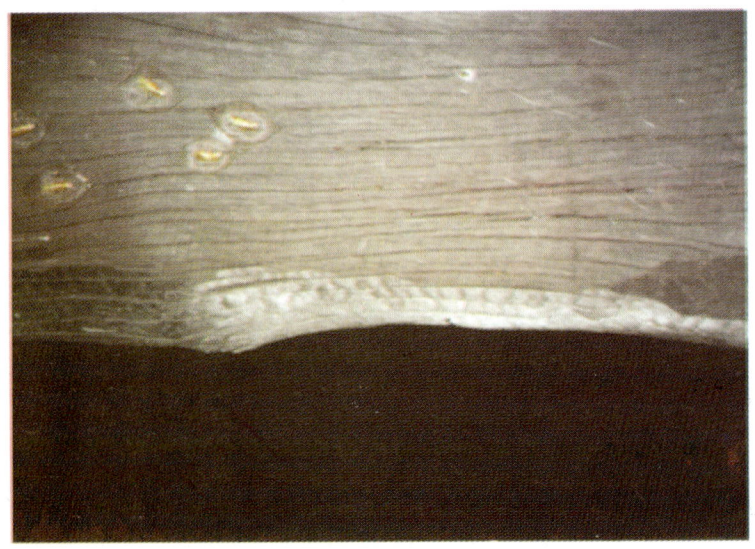

Insect larvae contained in super-fine, intricately woven

L to R, Col. H. B. Bisht, the author and Ronald Rosner

The Rodents

Large male tiger, about 400lbs, bounding across the Bauni

Lesser egret

The White Grass Plains

Lizard, 5in long, species unknown to author

Love

Magnificent tusker, in musth, visiting the author's camp

Massive vines encicrle and climb many of the trees of the WGP

The White Grass Plains

More than 50,000 people live around the WGP

Mugger croc on bank of upper Bauni, sun-bathing

The Rodents

Nest of the red ant, made of large leaves

Nesting enclosure of a dung beetle, some 36in below the surface

Nilghai Waterhole 11. IWCS project with AHF

One of many species of frog in the WGP

Paddy bird

Rare picture of a Fishing Cat, extremely shy and elusive

Remains of the old Bauni bridge built by the author

The Rodents

Repairing the Nilghai Waterhole 1 dam after a wild elephant visited

The Asian, or Indian One-Horned Rhino. Note the huge ears

The White Grass Plains

Sign at the main entrance to the reserve

Species of wasp in the WGP unknown to the author

Taru women fishnig with hand nets for edible fish, frogs etc

Terai rivers are mostly fordable in winter

The author's daughter, Rara, building a memorial to Mangal

The Rodents

Common House Rat, the Brown Rat, the Bandicoot Rat and the Alexandrine Rat. Also within the genus are the bamboo rats, of which there are two species, the Bay Bamboo Rat and the Hoary Bamboo Rat. The mice, which include four species, are the Indian Field Mouse, the Spiny Field Mouse, the Longtailed Tree Mouse and the House Mouse. And the voles, of which there are four species, consist of the Sikkim Vole, the Murree Vole, the Quetta Vole and Royle's Vole.

Then there are the flying squirrels. The larger members comprise the Kashmir Wooly Flying Squirrel, the Common Giant Flying Squirrel, the Large Brown Flying Squirrel, the Red Flying Squirrel and Hodgson's Flying Squirrel. And the smaller squirrels, which include the Lesser Giant Flying Squirrel, the Greyheaded Flying Squirrel, the Small Travancore Flying Squirrel, the Kashmir Flying Squirrel, the Particoloured Flying Squirrel and the Hairyfooted Flying Squirrel. And, lastly, the odd ones, the spiny ones, the porcupines, which number three species: the Indian Porcupine, Hodgson's and the Brushtailed Porcupine.

Of this fine gathering of rodentia, nineteen are found, or may be found, in the WGP. Already identified there by the author, or simply potential in habitat, they are as follows:

THE RED FLYING SQUIRREL, *P.p. albiventer* (Gray). Rana Taru: *pokra mousa*. Dangora Taru: *pakeri mousa*.

There are two races of the Common Giant Flying Squirrel. One is the Large Brown Flying Squirrel and the other is the Red Flying Squirrel. At least one, which is most probably the Red Flying Squirrel, is found in the WGP.

Flying squirrels are arboreal in habit, spending their lives high off the ground, living and breeding in trees. In the WGP the tree most commonly used as habitat is a tall, thin hardwood, the *sal* (*Shorea robusta*). Flying squirrels are not actually flying animals; they are gliders. (The only flying mammal is the bat.) Unlike other squirrels, they are nocturnal, rising from the day's roosting place in the early evening to seek food and returning again before dawn.

The little animal's limbs are linked with membranes of thin tissue and, when the animal is in movement, these open and act like the wings of a plane. Passage through the forest is generated by gliding from tree to tree. The direction of flight is a straight line but, because gravity is the power source of the animal's movement, it is always downwards. On arrival at the tree that is its chosen destination—where it will end its flight—the squirrel flares its membranes, lands, grabs on to the rough surface of the tree with its limbs and then races upwards to gain height for the next gliding leap.

Years ago, at one of my camps on the Bauni river, a pair lived in a *sal* tree at the edge of the campsite. Every evening they would come out and glide across the campsite, about 6–8ft above the ground, looking down, as though curious about the camp guests. They would do this several times and then leave to go foraging. After about a month they left the area permanently, probably because of the campfire smoke.

THE MALAYAN GIANT SQUIRREL, *Ratufa bicolor* (Sparrmann). Rana Taru: *pokra mousa*. Dangora Taru: *pakeri mousa*. Nepalese: *lokria*. Hindi: *karrat or rasu*.

Two species of squirrel common to India should also, one would think, be found in the forests of Nepal. But they are not. These are the Indian Giant Squirrel, which lives south of the Ganges, and the Grizzled Giant Squirrel, which is only found in south India and Sri Lanka. The single species of giant squirrel that is found in Nepal is the Malayan Giant Squirrel, and the author has seen one in the WGP. The animal is a deep brown in color, with buff-colored underparts. Adults measure 14–16in, with a tail of 24in.

Like most squirrels, the Malayan is a creature of the treetops, living alone, or in pairs, and seldom venturing to the ground. It can travel through the high foliage with superb physical ability, making leaps of up to 20ft. It is a very shy animal and is seldom seen. At the same time, it is noisy and its chattering call will often reveal its whereabouts to a keen observer. It shares with the monkeys a habit of calling in alarm at any sign of danger. If it feels threatened, rather than bolt, it may lie flat on the surface of a branch, or hide behind a tree trunk.

It is most active in its principal activity—hunting for food—in the early morning and late evening. Its lair, a large, balloon-like nest of small branches and leaves, is built at the outer ends of frail and slender branches, as a safeguard against tree-climbing predators.

THE FIVESTRIPED PALM SQUIRREL, *Funambulus pennanti* (Wroughton) and the THREESTRIPED PALM SQUIRREL, *Funambulus palmarum* (Linnaeus). Both animals: Rana Taru: *chita rengi*. Dangora Taru: *chidi mousa*. Nepalese: *lokherke*. Hindi: *gilheri*.

Both of these delightful, darting and super alert little creatures measure 5–6in in length, with tails of the same length. Both are brown in color, the Fivestriped being dark and the Threestriped much lighter, almost a fawn. The Fivestriped has five pale stripes on its back, three pale dorsal stripes on either side and a supplementary pale stripe. The Threestriped has three dorsal stripes and no supplementary lines.

The Fivestriped Palm Squirrel is an animal of mostly open country, but it is also found in villages and towns, where it will live in gardens, hedgerows and small trees. The Threestriped, on the other hand, is a creature of the forest. The food of both animals is nuts and fruits, buds and soft, fresh bark. They will drink the nectar of silk, cotton-tree blooms and, in this activity, assist in pollination. They also eat insects and the eggs of small birds, and will not hesitate to rob a nest to get these.

Males and females come together to mate for only a day or so in a year, during which time the female may mate with more than one male. While pregnant, the female builds a nest of twigs and leaves up above the ground, the Threestriped doing this in trees in the forest and the Fivestriped usually selecting the rafters of a house or barn, or holes in the walls of a building. The young are born blind and stay in the nest until they are capable of surviving on their own.

THE INDIAN GERBILLE *Tatera Indica*, (Hardwicke).

Having broad distribution in India, from the Himalaya to the tip of the peninsula, Cape Cormorin, the Indian Gerbille may well be found in the WGP. The gerbille belongs to a subdivision of the rat family and in appearance is somewhat similar. However, it is easily distinguishable from the hairless tailed rat by having an appendage that is covered with hair and usually ends in a tuft. Again, it has much longer hind legs; these allow for the typical progress of the little animal, which, unlike the walking or running pace of the rat, is in a series of kangaroo-like leaps and bounds.

Head and body, the Indian gerbille measures 6–7in. In coloration its coat is russet-brown to fawn or off-white fawn, and it has a light brown band running along each side of the tail. The little mammal is a burrowing rodent and makes its underground dens below bushes or thickets as well as in the open. Animals of different genders live in separate burrows; the burrow of the male gerbille has a single entrance, the female several. The entry tunnels descend to a sleeping chamber, the depth of which depends on the density of the soil of the area. From the chamber there is always a separate emergency exit passage, leading separately to the surface. The top of this passageway is normally covered and concealed with a thin crust of soil. In an emergency, such as to escape a predator, this is easily broken through by the hurriedly exiting owner.

Their food is grass, grain, roots, the fruit of wild plants, insects and their larvae, and the eggs and young of small ground-nesting birds. During harvest time they collect and store grain in their burrows.

THE INDIAN MOLE-RAT, *Bandicota bengalensis* (Gray and Hardwicke). Rana Taru: *gar mousa*. Dangora Taru: *bilkurua*.

This is a 6–9in long rodent, with a tail of about 6in. In color it is a dark grayish brown with dashes of buff; the undersides are paler. Although it looks like a bandicoot and is included in the bandicoot family, it is not a true bandicoot, that rodent being much larger. It does, however, have some of the habits of the bandicoot, one of which is erect hairs and grunting when disturbed. It is a burrowing animal; its habitat is both deciduous and evergreen forests, open country, towns and cities, where it advertises its presence with the molehill-like piles of soil it leaves around its burrows. From these comes its name, Mole-rat.

Its system of burrows is of considerable interest. A tunnel leads down about 24in to a central chamber, or gallery, which may vary in length from just a few feet to 60 feet. In the longer galleries, soil is thrown up to the surface in piles at intervals along the alignment of the chamber. These piles are visible to an above-ground observer but their sources are not, these being skillfully covered up and sealed by the rodent. Small round chambers are constructed along the sides of the gallery itself, the purpose of these being the storage of grain and other edible matter. Like the gerbille, the need for emergency exits is always included in the design of the burrows. In the case of the mole-rat, this includes several tunnels, all with their surface exits sealed with thin crusts of soil.

The mole-rat has an average life expectancy of about seven months. Males are sexually mature when eight weeks old, females are sexually active after fourteen weeks and the female can produce as many as seventy offspring in a calendar year. In some Indian cities the Mole-rat dominates all other rodents in numbers.

THE METAD or SOFTFURRED FIELD RAT, *Millardia meltada* (Gray).

The metad is a small, 5–6in rodent with a tail of the same length. The animal has dense, soft fur and large rounded ears; its coloration is light brown with grayish tones, the undersides a very light gray. Distribution covers all of peninsular India, from Uttar Pradesh—which borders on to the Nepal Terai—to southern India.

The animals live in pairs or small colonies in forest and scrubland; they will make their homes in rocks, stones and the broken walls of abandoned dwellings. Some make a small burrow in the roots of a bush or small tree; others are content to live in a pile of stones. Females produce litters two to seven times in a twelve-month period; the number of offspring per litter is between one and eight.

THE INDIAN BUSH RAT, *Golunda ellioti* (Gray).

This rat has a 4in body and a 4in tail. It has a rounded head, rounded ears and a hair covered tail. The fur is a yellowish brown dashed with black. Its habitat is mainly forest but it will also live in open country. Its lair is a thickly woven mass of twigs and grass and this may be built in a bush or built on the ground. It is an animal of slow movement and in its hunt for sustenance will follow the same paths with regularity, the result for a keen observer being highly visible narrow runways from its lair to its feeding areas. Its food is roots, grass and seeds. Like most rodents, it is highly prolific, no doubt designed by nature in this way to offset the high mortality rate it suffers from rodent-eating predators.

THE WHITETAILED WOOD RAT, Rattus blandfordi (Thomas).

The principal distribution of this rodent is central and eastern India. But it is also found in Bengal and so could conceivably be resident in the WGP. It measure 6–7in in length and has a long tail of some 8in or more. The animal's long, soft hair is gray is brown above and white below. Most distinctive is the coloration and markings of the tail; it is brown for three-quarters of its length but with a terminal segment covered with long white hairs.

The animal is mainly arboreal, spending much time in the trees, where presumably it finds much of its food. It makes its lair, a large messy collection of twigs and leaves, in a tree hollow or crack. Its young are born in June and October, 2–3 in a litter, and, like most rodents, it is not included in the lists of endangered species of our planet.

THE COMMON HOUSE RAT, Rattus rattus (Linnaeus) and the BROWN RAT, Rattus norvegicus (Berkenhout).

The Common House rat seems to be the most common species of the rat family. Its origin appears to have been in India and Burma, from where it traveled to propagate in all parts of the world. In coloration it varies through different regions, from black, to brown, to white-bellied. It is only the latter form that might be found in the WGP, in that its recorded distribution embraces both open country and forest. This is not so with the black form, which is a coastal creature, of sea ports, and the brown, which is limited in habitat to towns and cities. The Brown is actually classified as a separate species; it is a heavier-built rodent than the Common, with a shorter tail. However, it is not a forest dweller and therefore hardly to be found in the WGP. It seems to be confined mainly to areas of human habitation, where it seems to live quite happily in the noxious confines of drains, sewers and cesspits.

THE BANDICOOT RAT, *Bandicota Indica* (Bechstein).

This is by far the largest rat living in the Indian subcontinent and Nepal. When first encountered at close quarters, its size is quite startling, its body being a hefty 12–15in in length and its tail equally long. Its weight is 2–3lbs, making the creature almost twice as heavy as the normal rat. Though their habitat is mainly human dwellings in towns and villages, they will also live in open country, in brush and forest. They are omnivorous, like most of the genus, and the diet will include refuse, carrion, grain, fruit, vegetables, wild birds, small rodents and poultry. They are powerful burrowers and diggers, and have been known to bore through bricks and masonry to get at grain stores. They are highly destructive in domestic areas, especially to the floors and walls of dwellings; their large burrows signify their presence. Because of their size, they have fewer enemies than most smaller rodents, but because of the damage they inflict on human dwellings, barns and storage facilities, they are heavily persecuted by man. Nevertheless, with a fecundity that is inherent to their race, they survive in India, Nepal, Assam and Burma in uncountable numbers.

THE LONGTAILED TREE MOUSE, *Vandeleuria oleracea* (Bennett).

Although the author has never seen one, this attractive little mouse may very well live in the WGP, its distribution being all of the Indian peninsula. The animal has an unusually long tail and a body that measures 3–4in. Its soft fur is chestnut-colored and it has white underparts.

It is completely arboreal, and to this end nature has designed it to have the first and fifth toes of all four feet partially opposable

The Rodents

and ending in a flat nail, rather than a claw. Its tail is prehensile and using in climbing; its food is fruit, buds and delicate shoots.

When pregnant, the female makes a nest of whatever material she can find—leaves if they are available, grass if not. This is built into a hollow or crevice, high up in a tree, or in the branches of a tree. The little animal will also use the nests of other animals or birds. One is recorded as using a large spider's web in which to raise its young, apparently quite in harmony with the resident arachnids. Males build separate nests to use as sleeping quarters and do not attempt to occupy the nest of the birthing mother. Young are born three to six at a time; they will stay in the nest with the mother until they are capable of active and safe physical movement through the treetops.

THE SPINY FIELD MOUSE, *Mus platythrix* (Bennett). Rana and Dangora Taru: *moosa*.

This mouse is slightly larger than the Indian Field Mouse. Its fur is sandy to dark brown with white undersides, and the two areas are distinctly separate in coloration. The main difference is in its fur, almost all of which is made up of flattened spines. On the animal's back these are stiffer and rougher than those on the underparts. If these tiny animals are found in the WGP, they might live in hollow trees or logs, or in burrows. This is not known. But in dry and desert parts of India they burrow, with the design of their lairs embracing a quaint habit; after entering the burrow, as safeguard against predators, they close up the entrance, carefully blocking it with a collection of pebbles kept especially for this purpose.

THE INDIAN FIELD MOUSE, *Mus booduga* (Gray). Rana Taru: *moosa*. Dangora Taru: *kherkhaeti moosa*. Hindi: *moosa*.

This is one of the most common rodents of the Indian peninsula. It is 2–3in in length, with a tail of about 2in. In forested country the coloration is a grayish brown with white undersides, and in dry or desert terrain the dorsal fur is a pale sandy color. It has habitat everywhere, from forest and grassland to cities, towns and villages; it is equally at home in the outdoors or in houses. It is a highly prolific little animal and, although it is the prey of just about every flesh-eating predator that includes small mammals in its diet, which includes many of the snakes, it manages to survive successfully in millions.

THE HOUSE MOUSE, *Mus musculous* (Linnaeus). Rana and Dangora Taru: *gar ka moosa*. Hindi: *moosa*.

This little animal is the well-known house mouse of India, living in millions from the Himalaya of Nepal to the blue seas of the southern tip of India, Cape Cormorin. In size it measures 2–3in; it has a tail about the same length. Its color can vary from light to dark brown, with paler underparts. It is omnivorous and its principal habitat is human dwellings in villages, towns and cities. But it will also live in the open, in scrub, grassland and jungle, which means it may be found in the WGP.

The prey of a dozen or more rodent-eating predators, it spends its days searching for food, staying very alert to the possibility of being eaten by a predator and taking evasive action when needed. It is a very agile little animal and will climb vertical walls that are nearly smooth and appear to have no handholds; it will also leap considerable distances when alarmed. It has the extraordinary ability of squeezing through tiny cracks or holes that are sometimes only half the width of its body. It has a habit of using the same little trail over and over again; this is often visible to the eye of a keen observer. Its nest is usually made of soft materials, whatever it can find, including wool scraps, cotton balls, string and soft jungle debris. The nest is always tucked away in a secluded place; in dwellings this will be under floors or steps, in the dark corners of house attics and under furniture. In the wild, nests are hidden in holes in trees and logs, in crevices in stones and just about anywhere that offers seclusion and safety from predators.

Females mate and give birth 3–5 times a year, producing a brood of from 4–8 young at a time, each of the females of which can mate and give birth to the same number at the age of one month. In despair at what this means in terms of total numbers, I have to refer to my calculator to determine the number of offspring that this kind of fecundity will produce in a single year. The total is quite astounding.

BAY BAMBOO RAT, *Cannomys badius* (Hodgson) and the HOARY BAMBOO RAT, *Rhizomys pruinosus* (Blyth).

The Bamboo Rats, although rodents, are actually included in a separate family, the Rhizomyidae. Although their name suggests that they might be arboreal, spending their lives high in the leafy branches of bamboo growth, in actual fact they are subterranean creatures. The known distribution for both species is given as being from the Terai of Nepal all the way through Sikkim and Assam to Burma and beyond. This allows for habitat in the WGP.

The Bay measures 7–8in nose to tail, and the Hoary is a little larger, at 12–14in. In appearance like huge moles, the Bamboo Rats are distinguished by their big, protruding incisors. Their bodies are cylindrical in shape, with thick, short necks, short tails and short limbs armed with outsize claws. Coloration of the Bay is chestnut, and the Hoary is dark brown, with a grizzled coat. The movements of both animals are slow and, probably because of the amount of the time they spend underground, their eyesight is weak.

Both species live in burrows, which they excavate themselves. The tunnels run about 24in under the surface of the ground and terminate in a large chamber. Like some other rodents, the entrance to the burrow is closed up with dirt when it is occupied. The animals are nocturnal and herbivorous, their diet being grass, leaves and small roots, for which they dig energetically with their powerful claws. They are the prey of several predators, their only defense being a savage bite accompanied by a gnashing of their powerful incisors and much loud hissing.

THE INDIAN PORCUPINE, *Hystrix indica* (Kerr). Rana Taru: *sehi*. Dangora Taru: *sahi*. Nepalese: *dumchi*. Hindi: *sayal or sahi*.

The Indian Porcupine, an extraordinary example of nature's application of adaptability, measures, head and body, 28–35in, with a tail of 3–4in. The tail spines lengthen the appendage another 7–8in. Adults weigh from 25–40lbs. The animal's neck and shoulders are covered with a carpet of sharp, pointed bristles 6–12in in length. On the back there are two layers of bristles, a long, thin set hiding an undercoat of short thick spines. The quills are off-white in color and patterned with brown or black and white rings. The animal is both diurnal and nocturnal. Its lair is a hole in the ground, usually in a bank; it will either dig the hole itself or use one made by another animal. Entrances to the holes are very often strewn with bits and pieces of deer horn and sometimes bone. The animals gnaw on these; they contain calcium and lime, the consumption of which assists the growth of their quills. Though their main food is vegetables, fruit and grain of all kinds, at the same time they are the principal disposers of deer horn. In areas where the animals are plentiful, they are principally responsible for the fact that so very few horns are ever found. In the WGP the resident Swamp Deer herd shed probably one thousand sets of antlers every year, yet few are ever recovered.

When alarmed or annoyed, porcupines puff, grunt, erect their spines and rattle their long, hollow tail quills. For a small animal, they have unusual courage and, if they feel they are being threatened, and when it comes to flight or fight, they will quickly choose the latter and not hesitate to attack another animal in self-defense.

To protect themselves from a predator, they employ a very unusual tactic. This is to run backwards at the object of their ire at great speed, and clash violently with it in an effort to drive their erect quills in as deeply as possible. The results, for the attacker, will always be very painful and may in some cases be fatal. There is a record of a porcupine killing a leopard by driving its razor sharp spines into the big cat's head. They may also attack tigers. It is notable that many of the man-eating tigers recorded in north India and western Nepal, as recorded in my book, GENTLEMAN HUNTER, had porcupine quills deeply embedded in their bodies, injuries that in not a few cases disabled them and turned them into killer cats.

On impact with another animal, a porcupine's quills dislodge from the parent body to remain firmly embedded in the muscle and tissue of the animal's adversary. New quills quickly grow to replace damaged and lost ones. But the oft-repeated story that porcupines launch their spines at other animals—something which the Tarus believe, probably from the number of quills they find in the forest—is just a pleasant myth.

At this time the WGP seems to have a healthy population of these spiky and curious little creatures. They live in both the sal forest and the grasslands. Family raising is carried out by both parents, and the young, usually two to four, are born with their eyes open and their bodies covered with short, soft quills.

HODGSON'S PORCUPINE, *Hystrix hodgsoni* (Gray).

The habitat of this species is described as being Assam, southern Bengal and elevations of up to 5000 feet in the Himalaya. As the Terai, which contains the WGP, touches on to northern Bengal, there is some possibility that this species might be found in the WGP. No studies have been done to determine this. Hodgson's animal has a much lesser crest than the Indian; otherwise the two species are probably close to identical.

THE BRUSHTAILED PORCUPINE, *Atherurus macrourus* (Linnaeus).

Like Hodgson's Porcupine, the known habitat distribution of this animal allows to some extent for the possibility of its being found in the WGP. Its range on the subcontinent is Bengal and Assam, areas that in some parts at least have vegetation and ground cover similar to that of the WGP. This species differs from the Indian Porcupine in having a long tail ending in a singular, brush-like tuft of quills. It is generally considered to be rare and, no studies having been done, little is known about its breeding habits or its secretive lifestyle.

Porcupines are generally harmless to man. However, they seem to have a strong streak of curiosity about us; they will come into a camp at night and snuffle around, their presence indicated by the soft rustling of their bodies moving through the brush and the gentle clicking of their quills. Their curiosity extends itself to a little theft, now and then, and I have lost one perfectly good pair of boots to the animals. Left outside the tent overnight, they disappeared and signs on the ground indicated that they had been quietly removed by a *dumchi*. The signs also indicated that the little thief had firstly taken one boot, carted it off into the forest, then come back for the second one. I now sleep with my boots inside my tent!

THE BATS

There are twelve species of bat living in the Indian subcontinent, the Nepal Terai and the Nepal Himalaya. Of these, I have identified two in the WGP; these are the Flying Fox, the largest bat in Asia, and the Painted Bat. The remaining ten, all of which could be found in the WGP, are the Fulvous Fruit Bat, the Shortnosed Fruit Bat, the Bearded Sheathtailed Bat, the Indian False Vampire, the Great Eastern Horseshoe Bat, the Serotine, the Indian Pipistrelle, Tickell's Bat, the Great Himalayan Leafnosed Bat and the Common Yellow Bat.

THE FLYING FOX, *Pteropus giganteus* (Brunnich). Rana Taru: *chamgadar*. Dangora Taru: *gehedul*. Hindi: *Gadal or badur*.

This bat measures 9in in length, but has a huge wingspan of 48in, making it the largest bat in the Indo-Nepal region and possibly the largest bat in the world. It weighs almost 2lbs and its coloration includes a russet-red head with a black nose; its neck and shoulders are a pale brownish yellow, and the body behind the shoulders is dark brown or black. The wings are black.

The animal flies with a slow, heavy wingbeat. It nests in large noisy colonies high in trees, in forest and open country, as well as in towns and cities. They are found throughout Nepal and I have seen them in the WGP, though their roosting area was not determined. A large group has a permanent roost next to the king's residence in Katmandu, and they have been here for at least fifty years. In winter they migrate to roosts in the Terai, returning in the spring. Like most bats, the Flying Fox is affected by heat and cold; on very hot days in a roost they can be seen fanning themselves with one wing.

Flying Foxes leave their roosting trees half an hour after sunset every day and, flying in single file, follow the same routes, month after month, to their feeding grounds. It is said that they have an almost uncanny sense of when and where certain fruits are ripe and fly there at this opportune time to eat. The little mammal is a true fruit bat, but its food is the juice of fruits, which it chews; the fiber and pulp is discarded. It eats fruit where it finds it, but will also carry fruit back to the roost. This habit contributes to seed dispersal.

The Flying Fox seems to have few enemies; small predators on the whole avoid them. They do, however, suffer from parasitic flies, fleas and mites, which live in their fur and feed on the blood of their membranes. To rid themselves of these pests, they spend a lot of time, when roosting, combing their fur, using the claws of their feet and even their teeth.

The young are born blind, but with a thin coating of downy hair. They arrive in the world with a complete set of identical molar teeth, the single purpose of which, in the infant stage, is to grip and hold on to one of the mother's teats. They stay with their mother and fly with her until they are able to fend for themselves. She will leave them in the roost and fly off on her food forays without them. However, she will continue to feed them until they are fully able to feed themselves.

THE FULVOUS BAT, *Rousettus leschenaultia* (Desmarest).

This is a small bat with a head and body of just 5in and a tail of a little more than 0.5in. The coloration is light brown to yellow. Adult males have dull gray flanks when they are older. The young are naked at birth, pink in color, and are carried by the mother on her nocturnal flights for up to two months after birth. Juveniles reach adulthood within twelve months.

A highly gregarious mammal, they will roost in colonies of up to 2000 or more, their homes being in caves, manmade tunnels and old ruins, with darkness seemingly not necessary. They have unusually large and brilliant eyes.

When roosting, there does not seem to be segregation by gender in the colonies; juveniles, however, once free of the need of their mothers, will form separate groups. The Fulvous is a fruit bat and the need for food forces it to travel long distances. Like the Flying Fox, it retains an inbuilt memory of areas that produce fruit, as well as when it is ripe—it travels to and from these feeding grounds with a confident knowledge of their location.

THE SHORTNOSED FRUIT BAT, *Cynopterus sphinx* (Vahl).

Another small bat, a little less than 4.5in in length, with a tail of less than 0.5in. The almost hairless ears are margined in white and the nostrils are divergent. General coloration is different shades of brown, which in males is sometimes a bright reddish brown.

The little mammal is fairly common, but is not seen as much as many bats because of its habit of roosting singly or in small groups. Roosts are found mainly among palm tree leaves and the high roots of banyans, and rarely in caves. Foraging flights start early in the evening. Fruit is probably their principal food, but they will also sip nectar from flowers, flitting from blossom to blossom without settling, like an American Hummingbird. It will carry fruit back to a roost to eat and, because of this habit, contributes strongly to seed dispersal throughout its hunting terrain. Not much seems to be known about their social life or breeding habits, but the period of gestation is believed to be 115–125 days.

THE BEARDED SHEATHTAILED BAT, *Taphozous melanopogon* (Temminck).

A small, sandy-yellow bat with a black beard of long, thick hairs; females are brown with a russet tint. The young are a dark gray. Males grow the beard by which they are recognized at the age of six months. A fraction over 3in long, with a 1in tail, this little mammal is very gregarious and lives in colonies of from one hundred to as many as four thousand.

It has an unusual habit for a bat of not hanging by its hind legs; instead it clings to the walls of its roost, presumably caves, with all four limbs. If disturbed, it can move rapidly in any direction without leaving the wall. In the roost they do not segregate by sex but, when roosting, males usually occupy the outer limits of the colony.

They are insectivorous and usually leave the roost about half an hour after sunset, in fast-flying groups of from three to twelve. Mating time is in the months of January and February, and the gestation period is four months. Females give birth to a single offspring at a time; the infant bat is carried under the wing of the mother in a lateral position. It stays with the mother for a month and then leaves the parent. However, the mother will continue to suckle it in the roost for about another month.

THE INDIAN FALSE VAMPIRE, *Megaderma lyra* (Geoffroy).

This bat is both insectivorous and carnivorous. It is tailless and measures just over 3in in length. Coloration is a dark, ashy gray with pale underparts. The ears are big and rounded and the nose leaf has the appearance of being truncated.

The animal lives in small colonies of up to about 30; it makes its roosts in old buildings, caves and wells. Its food is large insects, including moths, but, being a carnivore, it will also kill and eat small animals, like other bats, mice, young rats, geckos, frogs and small birds like swallows and martins.

It flies close to the ground when hunting, and from a low altitude detects and kills small rodents. It will also pick its small prey off the face of vertical rock walls and cliffs.

In spite of the suggestive menace of its name, it is not dangerous to man. It mates in October and November; females give birth late in April, carrying their young until they are nearly fully-grown.

THE GREAT EASTERN HORSESHOE BAT, *Rhinolophus luctus* (Temminck).

The head and body of this species measures 3.55in in length and it has a tail of 2.6in. It is solid black in color, but some hairs have ashy tips. It has large ears that taper into blunt ends. The nose 'horseshoe' appendage is large, extends out over the lip and in the center is clearly incised.

It roosts alone, sometimes in pairs, in the split rock formations that are found throughout the nearly caveless Himalaya, and sometimes in old buildings. It hibernates in winter. In flight it is silent, but with heavy wing beats. It concentrates its hunting at an elevation of between 20ft–30ft above the ground.

THE GREAT HIMALAYAN LEAFNOSED BAT, *Hipposideros armiger* (Hodgson).

This species is slighter larger than the Eastern Horseshoe bat. Its coloration ranges from light to dark brown. It is supposedly only found in the Himalaya, but is included here as a 'possible' for the Terai and the WGP in that its range of elevation does not seem to be known.

THE SEROTINE, *Eptesicus serotinus* (Schreber).

The head and body measure 2.85in, with a tail of 2in. Above, it is a dark, smoky brown, with yellowish brown to white underparts. It has a flat head and ears of a moderate size.

Though found throughout the Himalaya, from Kashmir to Assam, it is not known if it has habitat in the Terai. It has a slow and butterfly-like flight and leaves its roosting place late in the evening. It roosts in tree hollows or holes in the walls of deserted buildings, both singly and in small groups. It hibernates in winter. It is believed that females give birth to one infant at a time. Apart from that, though the species is common in Europe, very little seems to be known about its lifestyle or breeding habits.

THE INDIAN PIPISTRELLE, *Pipistrellus coromandra* (Gray).

Measuring a diminutive 1.8in for its head and body, and with a tail of only 1.4in, the pipistrelle is one of the smallest of the bat family. Like so many of its brethren, it is dark brown above and paler below. The muzzle is short and thick and, in adults, furless up to the eyes. However, the top of the head and the forehead are thickly matted with fur. The ears are rounded at the tips.

It roosts in the roofs and eaves of domestic dwellings, and sometimes on the rough bark of trees. It leaves its diurnal roost earlier than most other bats and stays out all night, hunting and feeding, to return to the roost as little as fifteen minutes before dawn. It will enter dwellings in search of insects. Though its flight pattern is irregular, it is very fast and its extraordinary hunting capabilities are clearly demonstrated by the skill with which, in rapid flight, it catches and eats insects as small as flies.

It is believed to hibernate in winter but, like so many other bats, not a lot is known about its breeding habits.

TICKELL'S BAT, *Hesperoptenus tickelli* (Blyth).

This is a little-known member of the species, with a body of 2.6in and a tail of 2in. In color it is a pale yellowish gray; it has a gray head and at the base of each ear it has a tuft of whitish hair. It leaves its roost earlier than any of the genus and its flight is slow.

Its hunting and food-gathering territory is limited to the immediate vicinity of the roost. It is believed that it lies up during the day in tree hollows and crevices. Its mating time and gestation period seems to be unknown, but females are believed to give birth to a single young in May.

THE COMMON YELLOW BAT, *Scotophilus heathi* (Horsfield).

This species has a unique coloration of the underparts, which are bright canary yellow. The upper body is a yellowish brown, and among adults there is also a reddish variety, to the point where color, and also size, vary from animal to animal.

The animal makes its roosts in dwelling houses, in roofs and attics. It is gregarious and lives in moderately sized colonies. It is a noisy animal and spends much of its diurnal hours in chattering exchanges between groups and individuals. It commences its hunting early in the evening and flies in groups. It is an insectivorous bat and among its foods are flying ants.

It is said to hibernate in the northerly areas of its distribution. Females produce two young at a time, in June and July.

THE PAINTED BAT, *Kerivoula picta* (Pallas).

The coloration of this little bat makes it one of the most beautiful of the bat family. It also makes it easier to identify than other bats. Its color is a bright orange that reaches out along the fingers and the flanks. In contrast, the wing membranes are a solid black, with a speckling of tiny orange spots. The ears are funnel-shaped and it has a long, narrow and transparent tragus. Body measurements for the Painted Bat are given as 1.5in for its head and body, and 1.7in for its tail.

It roosts in dry leaves, the color of which helps to thoroughly camouflage the little animal; because of this, its diurnal roosts are hard to find. When roosting, it rests singly or in pairs. Its flight is described as being like that of a large moth, fluttery and erratic. I have seen this most attractive little bat several times in the WGP though I have not been able to find a roost. At this time there seems to be little information available on its lifestyle or breeding habits.

NOTE: In this section on bats, it will be noticed that only the Flying Fox has been allocated native names. Between Indians, Rana Tarus and Dangora Tarus, an in-depth study might show that the different species of bat are given different names. But on the whole, with native peoples, the three names—Rana Taru: chamgadar; Dangora Taru: gehedul; and Hindi: gadal or badur—the latter in my listing given to the Flying Fox, seem to be given to all species, regardless of species segregation.

THE BIRDS

The little Himalayan land of Nepal has a wonderful variety of birds, ranging from the tiniest, like the Velvet-fronted Nuthatch and the Pale-billed Flowerpecker, to birds with truly enormous wingspans, like the Himalayan Griffon.

The White Grass Plains reserve is blessed with no less than three hundred and fifty species, among which are some quite exotic ones, like the huge Eurasian Eagle Owl and the Bengal Florican. There are also some rare ones, like the Swamp Partridge and the Great Slaty Woodpecker.

I do not pretend to be an expert birder, my knowledge of the fauna of the WGP being mainly confined to its other wildlife. But ever since I first encountered the bird life of the Indian subcontinent in 1947, as a young tea planter in the Dooars district of North Bengal, I have been fascinated by their habits, their colors and the extraordinary number of their multitudinous species.

In the WGP, across the years, I have been privileged to enjoy the birdsong of many species. In my camps in the *phantas*, or up and down the Bauni River, I have awakened many times to the melodious calls of Black-headed Orioles and, in the evenings, to close down another long jungle day, the sweet sounds of Racquet-Tailed Drongos. I have heard the booming of the Great Hornbill and have been amused by the quaint wing movements, in flight, of it and its brother species—three flaps and a glide, three flaps and a glide. I have also been intrigued by the nesting habits of this bird,

The White Grass Plains

where the female, after conception, is sealed by the male in a hole in a tree and stays there until she lays her eggs.

For more than twenty years I have watched, from my winter camps on the Bauni River, the flight of a group of the subcontinent's largest woodpecker, the Great Slaty Woodpecker, flying every morning noisily up the east side of the Bauni, from somewhere in the south, to spend a day feeding in the *sal* forests of the park. I do not know the lifespan of this bird, but it is doubtful that the group that I have seen, winter after winter, are the same birds. This means that generations of them must be indoctrinated by their parents into following, for all of their lives, the same aerial flight routes.

In April, at the end of many a winter, camping in the open grassland of the *phantas*, I have been awakened at night by the plaintive calling of the migrating birds—among them Bar-headed and Greylag Geese, and many species of ducks, heading north to begin the tremendous climb that will take them over the Himalaya. To do this, they must fly at heights of not less than 15,000 feet and, for the Bar-Headed Geese, possibly as high as 23,000 feet—as certified by Lord Hunt, who heard them flying at night over his camp at 23,000 feet on the South Col during the 1953 Everest Expedition—to reach their nesting grounds in central and southern Asia. I have marveled that among them, flying with them to these incredible heights, is the little, fluttering, bumbling, short-winged Common Coot, a bird that in the wetlands of the WGP I have never seen fly more than fifty feet at a time.

I have also found, even as an amateur birdwatcher, that if one watches birds for a while, even though the books may tell you that pretty much all of their habits are known and explained, it is always possible to discover something new. So it was with a crow—a Large-Billed Crow—in the winter of 2004–2005, which started visiting me in camp and after a while became reasonably tame. One morning it arrived as usual just as I was finishing breakfast. It fixed its beady eyes on a small piece of toast that had fallen to the ground close to the breakfast table. Landing about ten feet away, it stood there for a moment and then, keeping its eyes firmly fixed on my face, commenced to walk *sideways*, using a perfect crab-like walk, for some fifteen feet, to where the piece of toast lay. There, with a quick snatch, it grabbed the toast and was then up and away with its prize! This is a bird whose normal terrestrial locomotion is walking and hopping, so to see it moving like this was fascinating.

The same thing can occur when you listen to birds. One morning in one of my safari camps, a group of us were having breakfast. We were sitting in the open, under the shade of a latticework of leafy vines that formed a huge tent over the camp. While we were talking quietly, and planning our day, I suddenly thought that I heard voices, human voices, come from somewhere nearby, something odd in a place where we were the only people. I signaled to the others to keep quiet for a moment and listen, and when they did this I quickly pinpointed the sounds. They were coming from directly above us and were being made by half a dozen Rufous Tree Pies. What they were doing was imitating, perfectly, what must have been, to them, the muted, murmuring sounds of our conversation as it came floating up to them from below.

One day in the not too distant future, I will be too old to go back to the WGP and once more enjoy the marvelous sights and sounds of the birds of the great forests; the strident morning calls of the *jungli murghi*—the Red Jungle Fowl; the raucous screams of circling Serpent Eagles, endlessly soaring on the warm, thermal air rising from the *phantas*, as they search for their prey; the childish-sounding chattering of the little brown Jungle Babblers—the Seven Sisters, as they are called—endlessly turning over the dry leaves of the jungle floor in search of grubs; the evening wailing of peafowl as they settle down for the night in their high perches at the tops of the giant silk cotton trees. And, throughout the night, from their nesting roosts along the banks of the Bauni River, the eerie, cackling, nocturnal screams of the Grey-headed Fish Eagles.

When the time comes and age prevents me from returning once more to enjoy the sylvan glades of the Terai forests, I shall miss those sounds.

To complete this dissertation on the birds of the WGP, a list of the known species of the park seems appropriate. However, when it comes to actually compiling this, and doing it well, with both correct naming and scientific classifications, I have to say that I find the task a little daunting. Thus I must fall back on an expert, in this case my Nepalese friend, Hem Bharal Ph.D. of Katmandu, Nepal who, in England in 2006, was the honored recipient of the prestigious Whitley Award. Here, with sincere thanks to Dr. Bharal, is the list.

Checklist of birds at Sukila Phanta

Key to Checklist

r resident, **br** breeding confirmed resident, **w** winter, **m** migrant, **s** summer, **1** common, **2** fairly common, **3** occasional, **4** uncommon, **5** rare

English Name *Scientific Name* **Status**

GREBES, *Podicipediae*
Little grebe *Tachybaptus ruficollis* r, w?, 3

CORMORANTS, *Pelecanidae*
Great cormorant *Phalacrocorax carbo* w, 2
Little cormorant *Phalacrocorax niger* br, 1

ANHINGAS, *Anhingidae*
Oriental darter *Anhinga melanogaster* br, 2

HERONS & BITTERNS, Ardeidae
Yellow bittern *Ixobrychus sinensis* sbr, 3
Cinnamon bittern *Ixobrychus cinnamomeus* r, s, 3
Black bittern *Dupetor flavicollis* r, 4
Black-crowned night heron *Nycticorax nycticorax* br, 3
Green-backed heron *Butorides striatus* r, 2
Indian pond heron *Ardeola grayii* br, 1
Cattle egret *Bubulcus ibis* br, 1
Little egret *Egretta garzetta* br, 1
Intermediate egret *Egretta intermedia* br, 2
Great egret *Egretta alba* br, 2
Grey heron *Ardea cinerea* w, 3
Purple heron *Ardea purpurea* br, 1

STORKS, Ciconiidae
Painted stork *Mycteria leucocephala* s, r?, 4
Asian openbill stork *Anastomas oscitans* r, 3
Black stork *Ciconia nigra* w, 3
Woolly-necked stork *Ciconia episcopus* r, 2
White stork *Ciconia ciconia* w?, m, 5
Black-necked stork *Ephippiorrhynchus asiaticus* w, r?, 3
Lesser adjutant stork *Leptoptilos javanicus* br, 2

IBISES & SPOONBILLS, Threskiornithidae
Red-naped ibis *Pseudibis papillosa* br, 1

SWANS, GEESE & DUCKS, Anatidae
Lesser whistling duck *Dendrocygna javanica* r, 2
Bar-headed goose *Anser indicus* w, m, 3
Ruddy shelduck *Tadorna ferruginea* w, 2
Cotton pygmy goose *Nettapus coromandelianus* r, s, 2
Eurasian wigeon *Anas penelope* w, m, 3
Falcated duck *Anas falcata* w, m, 4
Gadwall *Anas strepera* w, m, 1
Mallard *Anas platyrhynchos* w, m, 1

The White Grass Plains

Spotbill *Anas poecilorhyncha* w, r?, 3
Common teal *Anas crecca* w, m, 1
Garganey *Anas querquedula* w, m, 3
Northern pintail *Anas acuta* w, m, 2
Northern shoveler *Anas clypeata* w, m, 3
Red-crested pochard *Netta rufina* w, m, 4
Common pochard *Aythya ferina* w, m, 3
Ferrugionus duck *Aythya nyroca* w, m, 3
Tufted duck *Aythya fuligula* w, m, 3

HAWKS, EAGLES & VULTURES, Accipitridae

Crested honey buzzard *Pernis ptilorhyncus* r, 1
Black-shouldered kite *Elanus caeruleus* r, w?, 2
Pariah kite *Milvus migrans* r, w, 2
Brahminy kite *Haliastur indus* w, 4
Pallas's fishing eagle *Haliaeetus leucoryphus* br?, m, 5
Lesser fishing eagle *Ichthyophaga nana* r?, 4
Grey-headed fishing eagle *Ichthyophaga ichthyaetus* r, 2
Egyptian vulture *Neophron percnopterus* r?, w, 3
Oriental white-backed vulture *Gyps bengalensis* br, 1
Long-billed vulture *Gyps indicus* br, 1
Eurasian griffon vulture *Gyps fulvus* w, 2
Red-headed vulture *Sarcogyps calvus* w, 3
Eurasian black vulture *Aegypius monachus* w, 4
Short-toed eagle *Circaetus gallicus* w, 3
Crested serpent eagle *Spilornis cheela* r, 1
Eurasian marsh harrier *Circus aeruginosus* w, 2
Hen harrier *Circus cyaneus* w, 2
Pallid harrier *Circus macrourus* w, m, 4
Montagu's harrier *Circus pygargus* w, m, 5
Pied harrier *Circus melanoleucos* w, m, 3
Besra *Accipiter virgatus* r?, 3
Shikra *Accipter badius* br, 2
White-eyed buzzard *Butastur teesa* r, 2
Common buzzard *Buteo buteo* w, 3

Lesser spotted eagle *Aquila pomarina* r, 3
Greater spotted eagle *Aquila clanga* w, m, 4
Steppe eagle *Aquila nipalensis* w, m, 2
Tawny eagle *Aquila vindhiana* r, 4
Booted eagle *Hieraaetus pennatus* w, 4
Bonelli's eagle *Hieraaetus fasciatus* w, 4
Changeable hawk eagle *Spizaetus cirrhatus* r, 2

OSPREY, *Pandionidae*
Osprey *Pandion haliaetus* w, 3

FALCONS, *Falconidae*
Red-thighed falconet *Microhierax caerulescens* w?, 5
Lesser kestrel *Falco naumanni* w, m, 4
Common kestrel *Falco tinnunculus* w, 3
Eurasian hobby *Falco subbuteo* s, 4
Peregrine falcon *Falco peregrinus* w, m, 4

FRANCOLINS & PHEASANTS, *Phasianidae*
Black francolin *Francolinus francolinus* br, 1
Swamp francolin *Francolinus gularis* br, 2
Common quail *Coturnix coturnix* w, m, 5
Blue-breasted quail *Conturnix chinensis* r?, 5
Red jungle fowl *Gallus gallus* br, 1
Blue peafowl *Pavo cristatus* br, 1

HEMIPODES, *Turnicidae*
Striped buttonquail *Turnix sylvatica*
Yellow-legged buttonquail *Turnix tanki*
Barred buttonquail *Turnix suscitator* r, 4

RAILS, COOTS & GALLINULES, *Rallidae*
Ruddy-breasted crake *Porzana fusca* r, 3
Brown crake *Amaurornis akool* r, 5
White-breasted waterhen *Amaurornis phoenicurus* br, 1
Common moorhen *Gallinula chloropus* w, 1

Purple gallinule *Porphyrio porphyrio* r, w, 2
Common coot *Fulica atra* w, 2

CRANES, *Gruidae*
Sarus crane *Grus antigone* r?, m, 5
Demoiselle crane *Anthropoides virgo* m, 5

FLORICANS, *Otidae*
Lesser florican *Sypheotides indica* s, 5
Bengal florican *Houbaropsis bengalensis* r, 2

JACANAS, Jacanidae
Pheasant-tailed jacana *Hydrophasianus chirurgus* r, s, 3
Bronze-winged jacana *Metopidius indicus* br, 2

PAINTED SNIPE, *Rostratulidae*
Painted snipe *Rostratula benghalensis* r, 3

STILT, *Recurvirostridae*
Black-winged stilt *Himantopus himantopus* m, 5

STONE CURLEW, *Burhinidae*
Northern stone-curlew *Burhinus oedicnemus* r, 3

COURSER AND PRATINCOLES, *Glareolidae*
Indian courser *Cursorius coromandelicus* w, r?, 5
Oriental pratincole *Glareola maldivarum* s, 4
Little pratincole *Glareola lactea* r, 3

PLOVERS AND LAPWINGS, *Charadriidae*
Little ringed plover *Charadrius dubius* r?, w, 2
River lapwing *Hoplopterus duvaucelii* r, 2
Yellow-wattled lapwing *Hoplopterus malabaricus* r, 3
Red-wattled lapwing *Hoplopterus indicus* br, 1
Northern lapwing *Vanellus vanellus* w, m, 3

SANDPIPERS, *Scolopacidae*
Temminck's stint *Calidris temminckii* w, m, 2
Long-toed stint *Calidris subminuta* w, 5
Ruff *Philomachus pugnax* m, 5
Common snipe *Gallinago gallinago* w, m, 2
Spotted redshank *Tringa erythropus* m, 4
Common redshank *Tringa totanus* w, m, 3
Marsh sandpiper *Tringa stagnatilis* m, 4
Common greenshank *Tringa nebularia* w, m, 1
Green sandpiper *Tringa ochropus* w, m, 1
Wood sandpiper *Tringa glareola* w, m, 2
Common sandpiper *Actitis hypoleucos* w, m, 1

TERNS, *Laridae*
River tern *Sterna aurantia* r, 2
Black-bellied tern *Sterna acuticauda* r, 2

PIGEONS & DOVES, *Columbidae*
Blue rock pigeon *Columba livia* r?, w, 2
Eurasian collared dove *Streptopelia decaocto* br, 1
Red turtle dove *Streptopelia tranquebarica* br, 2
Oriental turtle dove *Streptopelia orientalis* w, 2
Spotted dove *Streptopelia chinensis* br, 1
Emerald dove *Chalcophaps indica* br, 1
Orange-breasted green pigeon *Treron bicincta* r, 2
Pompadour green pigeon *Treron pompadoura* r, 2
Yellow-footed green pigeon *Treron phoenicoptera* r, 2

PARAKEETS, *Psittacidae*
Alexandrine parakeet *Psittacula eupatria* br, 1
Ring-necked parakeet *Psittacula krameri* br, 1
Slaty-headed parakeet *Psittacula himalayana* w, 4
Plum-headed parakeet *Psittacula cyanocephala* br, 1
Moustached parakeet *Psittacula alexandri* r, 5

The White Grass Plains

CUCKOOS, Cuculidae
Pied crested cuckoo *Clamator jacobinus* s, 4
Red-winged crested cuckoo *Clamator coromandus* s, 4
Common hawk cuckoo *Hierococcyx varius* r, 1
Indian cuckoo *Cuculus micropterus* s, 1
Common cuckoo *Cuculus canorus* s, 2
Drongo cuckoo *Surniculus lugubris* s, 3
Common koel *Eudynamys scolopacea* s, 2
Large green-billed malkoha *Phaenicophaeus tristis* r, 4
Sirkeer malkoha *Phaenicophaeus leschenaultii* r, 2
Greater coucal *Centropus sinensis* br, 1
Lesser coucal *Centropus bengalensis* r, s, 2

OWLS, Strigidae
Grass owl *Tyto capensis* r?, 5
Indian scops owl *Otus bakkamoena* r, 3
Oriental scops owl *Otus sunia* r, 2
Collared scops owl *Otus lempiji* r, 2
Dusky eagle owl *Bubo coromandus* r, 3
Spot-bellied eagle owl *Bubo nipalensis* r?, w, 4
Brown fish owl *Ketupa zeylonensis* r, 2
Jungle owlet *Glaucidium radiatum* r, 1
Asian barred owlet *Glaucidium cuculoides* r, 5
Brown hawk owl *Ninox scutulata* r, 2
Spotted owlet *Athene brama* br, 2

NIGHTJARS, Caprimulgidae
Savanna nightjar *Caprimulgus affinis* s, 2
Indian nightjar *Caprimulgus asiaticus* r?, 3
Large-tailed nightjar *Caprimulgus macrurus* r, 2

SWIFTS, Apodidae
Himalayan swiftlet *Collocalia brevirostris* w, 3
White-rumped needletail *Zoonavena sylvatica* r, 3
Alpine swift *Apus melba* w, 3
Little swift *Apus affinis* r, 2

The Birds

TREESWIFTS, *Hemiprocnidae*
Crested treeswift *Hemiprocne coronata* r, 2

KINGFISHERS, *Alcedinidae*
White-breasted kingfisher *Halcyon smyrnensis* br, 1
Stork-billed kingfisher *Pelargopsis capensis* br, 1
Common kingfisher *Alcedo atthis* br, 1
Deep-blue kingfisher *Alcedo meninting* r?, 4
Pied kingfisher *Ceryle rudis* r, 2

BEE-EATERS, *Meropidae*
Blue-bearded bee-eater *Nyctyornis athertoni* r, 4
Green bee-eater *Merops orientalis* br, s, 2
Blue-tailed bee-eater *Merops philippinus* s, 2
Chestnut-headed bee-eater *Merops leschenaulti* s, 3

ROLLERS, *Coraciidae*
Indian roller *Coracias benghalensis* br, 1
Dollar bird *Eurystomus orientalis* s, 3

HOOPOES, *Upupidae*
Hoopoe *Upupa epops* r?, w, 2

HORNBILLS, *Bucerotidae*
Indian grey hornbill *Tockus birostris* r, 2
Oriental pied hornbill *Anthracoceros coronatus* r, 1

BARBETS, *Capitonidae*
Lineated barbet *Megalaima lineata* r, 4
Brown-headed barbet *Megalaima zeylanica* r, 1
Coppersmith barbet *Megalaima haemacephala* br, 2

WRYNECKS, *Jyngidae*
Eurasian wryneck *Jynx torquilla* w, 3

WOODPECKERS, *Picidae*
Rufous woodpecker *Celeus brachyurus* r, 3
Lesser yellow-naped woodpecker *Picus chlorolophus* r, 2

The White Grass Plains

Greater yellow-naped woodpecker *Picus flavinucha* r?, 4
Grey-headed woodpecker *Picus canus* r, 2
Streak-throated green woodpecker *Picus myrmecophoneus* br, 1
Himalayan golden-backed woodpecker *Dinopium shorii* r, 2
Lesser golden-backed woodpecker *Dinopium benghalense* r, 1
Greater golden-backed woodpecker *Chrysocolaptes lucidus* r, 2
White-naped woodpecker *Chrysocolaptes festivus* r, 3
Bay woodpecker *Blythipicus pyrrhotis* v
Great slaty woodpecker *Mulleripicus pulverulentus* r, 3
Yellow-crowned pied woodpecker *Dendrocopos mahrattensis* r, 3
Brown-capped pigmy woodpecker *Dendrocopos moluccensis* br, 1

PITTAS, *Pittidae*
Indian pitta *Pitta brachyura* s, 4

LARKS, *Alaudidae*
Singing bushlark *Mirafra cantillans* s, r?, 4
Bengal bushlark *Mirafra assamica* r, 2
Ashy-crowned finchlark *Eremopterix grisea* r, 2
Rufous-tailed Lark *Ammomanes phoenicurus* w?, 5
Sandlark *Calendrella raytal* r, 1
Oriental skylark *Alauda gulgula* br, 1

SWALLOWS, *Hirundinidae*
Pale martin *Riparia diluta* s, r?, 3
Brown-throated sand martin *Riparia paludicola* br, 1
Barn swallow *Hirundo rustica* r, w, 1
Red-rumped swallow *Hirundo daurica* r, 2
Streak-throated swallow *Hirundo fluvicola* s, r?, 3
Nepal house martin *Delichon nipalensis* w, 4
Asian house martin *Delichon dasypus* w, 5

WAGTAILS & PIPITS, *Motacillidae*
Richard's pipit *Anthus richardi* w, 3
Paddyfield pipit *Anthus rufulus* br, 1
Tawny pipit *Anthus campestris* w, 4

The Birds

Long-billed pipit *Anthus similis* w, 3
Olive-backed pipit *Anthus hodgsoni* w, 2
Tree pipit *Anthus trivialis* w, m, 4
Rosy pipit *Anthus roseatus* w, 2
Yellow wagtail *Motacilla flava* w, m, 3
Citrine wagtail *Motacilla citreola* w, m, 2
Grey wagtail *Motacilla cinerea* w, 3
Pied/White wagtail *Motacilla alba* w, 1
White-browed wagtail *Motacilla maderaspatensis* br, 2

CUCKOOS-SHRIKES, *Campephagidae*
Common woodshrike *Tephrodornis pondicerianus* r, 2
Bar-winged flycatcher-shrike *Hemipus picatus* r, 2
Black-winged cuckoo-shrike *Coracina melaschistos* r, 3
Large cuckoo-shrike *Coracina novaehollandiae* r, 1
Scarlet minivet *Pericrocotus flammeus* r, 2
Long-tailed minivet *Pericrocotus ethologus* w, 2
Small minivet *Pericrocotus cinnamomeus* r, 1

BULBULS, *Pycnonotidae*
Black-crested yellow bulbul *Pycnonotus melanicterus* r, 3
Red-whiskered bulbul *Pycnonotus jocosus* br, 1
Red-vented bulbul *Pycnonotus cafer* br, 1

LEAFBIRDS, *Irenidae*
Common iora *Aegithina tiphia* r, 1
Golden-throated leafbird *Chloropsis aurifrons* r, 3

THRUSHES, *Turdidae*
Siberian rubythroat *Luscinia calliope* w, m, 4
White-tailed rubythroat *Luscinia pectoralis* w, 3
Bluethroat *Luscinia svecica* w, m, 1
Asian magipe-robin *Copsychus saularis* br, 1
White-rumped shama *Copsychus malabaricus* br, 2
Black redstart *Phoenicurus ochruros* w, m, 3
Common stonechat *Saxicola torquata* w, 1

White-tailed stonechat *Saxicola leucura* br, 1
White-throated bushchat *Saxicola insignis* w, 2
Pied bushchat *Saxicola caprata* br, 1
Jerdon's bushchat *Saxicola jerdoni* br, 3
Grey bushchat *Saxicola ferrea* w, 2
Northern wheatear *Oenanthe oenanthe* w?, m, 5
Desert wheatear *Oenanthe deserti* w?, m, 5
Variable wheatear *Oenanthe picata* w?, m, 5
Indian robin *Saxicoloides fulicata* r, 3
Blue whistling thrush *Myiophoneus caeruleus* w, 3
Scaly thrush *Zoothera dauma* w, 3
Orange-headed thrush *Zoothera citrina* s, r?, 2
Tickell's thrush *Turdus unicolor* w, 3
Dark-throated thrush *Turdus ruficollis* w, 3

WARBLERS, Sylviidae
Grey-bellied tesia *Tesia cyaniventer* w, 5
Pale-footed bush warbler *Cettia pallidipes* r?, 5
Aberrant bush warbler *Cettia flavolivacea* w, 1
Grey-sided bush warbler *Cettia brunnifrons* w, m, 2
Spotted bush warbler *Bradypterus thoracicus* w, 3
Brown bush warbler *Bradypterus luteoventris* v?
Bright-capped cisticola *Cisticola exilis* br, 1
Fantail cisticola *Cisticola juncidis* br, 1
Plain prinia *Prinia inornata* br, 2
Ashy prinia *Prinia socialis* br, 3
Grey-breasted prinia *Prinia hodgsoni* br, 1
Yellow-bellied prinia *Prinia flaviventris* br, 2
Jungle prinia *Prinia sylvatica* br, 3
Graceful prinia *Prinia gracilis* r?, 3
Large grass warbler *Graminicola bengalensis* br, 1
Common tailorbird *Orthotomus sutorius* br, 1
Lanceolated warbler *Locustella lanceolata* w, m, 5
Bristled grass warbler *Chaetornis striatus* s, r?, 2
Striated marsh warbler *Megalurus palustris* br, 2

The Birds

Paddyfield Warbler *Acrocephalus agricola* w, m, 4
Blyth's reed warbler *Acrocephalus dumetorum* w, m, 1
Thick-billed Warbler *Acrocephalus aedon* w, m, 4
Moustached Warbler *Acrocephalus melanopogon* m, 5
Booted warbler *Hippolais caligata* w, 3
Orphean warbler *Sylvia hortensis* m, 5
Lesser whitethroat *Sylvia curruca* pm, w, 5
Golden-spectacled warbler *Seicercus burkii* pm, w, 4
Whistler's Warbler *Seicercus whistleri* w, 2
Grey-hooded warbler *Seicercus xanthoschitos* w, 3
Blyth's crowned warbler *Phylloscopus reguloides* w, 1
Greenish warbler *Phylloscopus trochiloides* w, 2
Pallas's leaf warbler *Phylloscopus proregulus* w, 3
Yellow-browed warbler *Phylloscopus inornatus* w, 2
Dusky warbler *Phylloscopus fuscatus* w, m, 3
Smoky warbler *Phylloscopus fuliginventer* w, 2
Sulphur-bellied warbler *Phylloscopus griseolus* m, 5
Tickell's warbler *Phylloscopus affinis* w,m, 3
Chiffchaff *Phylloscopus collybita* w, m, 2

FLYCATCHERS, Muscicapidae

Pale-chinned flycatcher *Cyornis poliogenys* s, r?, 4
Blue-throated blue flycatcher *Cyornis rubeculoides* w?, 4
Tickell's blue flycatcher *Cyornis tickelliae* r, 3
Verditer flycatcher *Muscicapa thalassina* w, 3
Asian sooty flycatcher *Muscicapa sibirica* m, 4
Rufous-tailed flycatcher *Muscicapa ruficauda* w, 4
Slaty blue flycatcher *Ficedula tricolor* w, 2
Ultramarine flycatcher *Ficedula superciliaris* w, 3
Little pied flycatcher *Ficedula westermanni* w, 5
Snowy-browed flycatcher *Ficedula hyperythra* w, 5
Orange-gorgetted flycatcher *Ficedula strophiata* w, 4
Red-breasted flycatcher *Ficedula parva* w, 2
Grey-headed flycatcher *Culicicapa ceylonensis* w, 2
Yellow-bellied fantail *Rhipidura hypoxantha* w, 3

The White Grass Plains

White-throated fantail *Rhipidura albicollis* r, 2
White-browed fantail *Rhipidura aureola* r, 4
Asian paradise flycatcher *Terpsiphone paradisi* s, r, 3
Black-naped monarch *Hypothymis azurea* s, r?, 3

BABBLERS, *Timaliidae*
Puff-throated babbler *Pellorneum ruficeps* r, 5
Rufous-bellied babbler *Dumetia hyperythra* r, 3
Striped tit-babbler *Macronous gularis* r, 3
Red-capped babbler *Timalia pileata* br, 1
Yellow-eyed babbler *Chrysomma sinense* br, 2
Jerdon's babbler *Chrysomma altirostre* r, 5
Striated babbler *Turdoides earlei* br, 1
Jungle babbler *Turdoides striatus* br, 1

TITMICE, *Paridae*
Great tit *Parus major* br, 1

NUTHATCHES, *Sittidae*
Velvet-fronted nuthatch *Sitta frontalis* r?, 5
Chestnut-bellied nuthatch *Sitta castanea* br, 1

SUNBIRDS, *Nectariniidae*
Purple sunbird *Nectarinia asiatica* br, 1
Crimson sunbird *Aethopyga siparaja* r, 4

FLOWERPECKERS, *Dicaeidae*
Thick-billed flowerpecker *Dicaeum agile* r, 2
Pale-billed flowerpecker *Dicaeum erythrorhynchos* r, 3

WHITE-EYES, *Zosteropidae*
Oriental white-eye *Zosterops palpebrosa* br, 1

ORIOLES, Oriolidae
Black-hooded oriole *Oriolus xanthornus* br, 1
Eurasian golden oriole *Oriolus oriolus* s, 3

The Birds

SHRIKES, *Laniidae*
Brown shrike *Lanius cristatus* w, 3
Bay-backed shrike *Lanius vittatus* w, m, 4
Long-tailed shrike *Lanius schach erythronotus* r, 1
Grey-backed shrike *Lanius tephronotus* w, 3

DRONGOS, *Dicruridae*
Black drongo *Dicrurus macrocercus* r, 1
Ashy drongo *Dicrurus leucocephaeus* s, 2
White-bellied drongo *Dicrurus caerulescens* r, 1
Lesser racket-tailed drongo *Dicrurus remifer* w, 4
Spangled drongo *Dicrurus hottentottus* r, 3
Greater racket-tailed drongo *Dicrurus paradiseus* r, 1

WOOD SWALLOWS, *Artamidae*
Ashy wood swallow *Artamus fuscus* r, 3

CROWS & JAYS, *Corvidae*
Red-billed blue magpie *Urocissa erythrorhyncha* r?, 4
Rufous tree pie *Dendrocitta vagabunda* r, 1
House crow *Corvus splendens* r, 2
Jungle crow *Corvus macrorhynchos* r, 1

STARLINGS, *Sturnidae*
Spot-winged Starling *Sturnus spiloptera* w, m, 3
Chestnut-tailed starling *Sturnus malabaricus* r, 2
Brahminy starling *Sturnus pagodarum* r, 3
Eurasian starling *Sturnus vulgaris* w, m, 2
Asian pied starling *Sturnus contra* r, 2
Common mynah *Acridotheres tristis* r, 2
Bank mynah *Acridotheres ginginianus* r, 2
Jungle mynah *Acridotheres fuscus* r, 1
Hill mynah *Gracula religiosa* r, 4

WEAVERS, *Ploceidae*
House sparrow *Passer domesticus* r, 3
Yellow-throated sparrow *Petronia xanthocollis* r, 1

Black-breasted weaver *Ploceus benghalensis* r, 1
Streaked weaver *Ploceus manyar* r?, 4
Baya weaver *Ploceus philippinus* r, 1
Finn's weaver *Ploceus megarhynchus* r, 3

MUNIAS, *Estrildidae*
Red avadavat *Amandava amandava* br, 1
Scaly-breasted munia *Lonchura punctulata* br, 1
Chestnut munia *Lonchura malacca* r, 5

FINCHES & ALLIES, *Fringillidae*
Yellow-breasted greenfinch *Carduelis spinoides* w, 2
Common rosefinch *Carpodacus erythrinus* w, 1

BUNTINGS, *Emberizidae*
Yellow-breasted bunting *Emberiza aureola* w, 1
Chestnut-eared bunting *Emberiza fucata* w, 3
Crested bunting *Melophus lathami* w, 1

THE FISHES

The rivers and lakes of the White Grass Plains have an extraordinary number of species of fish for such a small area and such a limited number of rivers. The Nepalese ichthyologists list twenty-seven species in all.

Whereas my interest in wildlife began as a hunter and continued as a conservationist, my fascination with fishes is, I have to admit, as a keen angler, one whose lifetime dedication to the challenge of sport fishing began as a boy in the lakes and rivers of Ireland. From there I branched out, as time and travel allowed, to barracuda fishing in the Cocos Keeling islands of the Indian Ocean, shark fishing off Thursday Island in Australia's magnificent Barrier Reef, the Indian Ocean off Sri Lanka, and the Burrampooter, in upper Assam and north Bengal. There, as a tea planter in the fifties, I ardently fished all the great rivers that poured out of the foothills of the eastern Himalaya—from the mighty Teesta, with its origins in northern Sikkim, to the Toorsa, out of eastern Bhutan. And, as we used to say, all the rivers in between, including what was for me a local river, the Jaldaka of the Nagrakata district, where, on any sunny morning, I could pick up a nice three-pound *mahseer* or a fine, fat *cutley* for lunch. Also Rara Lake, in the middle western Himalaya in Nepal, hard under the rugged mountains of the Kanjiroba Himal, to collect, on behalf of the Philadelphia Academy of Natural Sciences, the unknown fish of the deep, crystal clear waters of a lake so beautiful that I named my daughter after it.

The White Grass Plains

I began fishing the WGP in the fifties and the river that I concentrated on was the Bauni. The Sarda, to the west, is a much bigger river, but where it borders the WGP it is shallow and stony. One has to go far up its course to find deep water and big fish, the fish in question of course being the mighty *mahseer*, the great fighting fish of the lower Himalayan rivers. The same pretty much applies to the other rivers of the reserve, all of which are shallow with nothing to offer a sportsman but small fish. The Bauni, however, has water deep enough in several places to hold large fish—two of its deepest holes are one mile north, and one mile south, respectively, of the Bauni bridge.[4]

For a sport fisherman, the fish of the Bauni provide many hours of enjoyment. All of the bigger fish are very wily and, whereas on arrival of the fisherman at the river, they may be seen chasing fry up to and out of the surface, as soon as they detect the presence of what they consider danger—a person— they will go straight to the bottom and stay there until the fisherman has gone, or at least until he has waited long enough in concealment to convince them that it is safe to come up again. This indicates acute above-surface vision and an awareness of hazards of predators such as Fish Eagles, of which the Bauni has a resident population.

Again, when they are hooked, they will invariably dive straight to the bottom and endeavor to get into the dense lair of debris that covers it in the form of fallen trees and brush. Once in there, all attempts to get them out will fail. So, once hooked, if the fisherman cannot control and prevent this sudden, powerful plunge into the depths and the safety that it offers, the fish will be lost.

---

[4] In the winter of 2002, with a grant from the American Himalayan Foundation and as part of a long-term project by IWCS to enhance fish habitat in the Bauni, an existing fish hole immediately north of the bridge was dug out and deepened. As of 2007, further deepening work is planned in an effort to provide additional breeding habitat for the larger fish.

The Fishes

Even if the fish can be prevented from getting into the bottom maze of dead logs and tangled branches, and held in the intervening water, then it will still put up a great fight. Eventually, if properly played, it will allow itself to be drawn into the bank and picked up. This latter is best done with a gaff, for many of the Bauni fish—unlike the *mahseer* of the hill rivers, the teeth of which are set in their throats—have wicked sets of small sharp teeth set in their mouths designed especially to bite the hand of the unwary angler painfully.

The fish of all countries have their mysteries, the principal of which always seem to revolve around their feeding patterns. The Bauni fish seem to feed at all hours of the day and even into the night, but there are times when they do not seem to feed at all. Of course this will be one or more of the many times one is on the river trying to catch one! So, although I have fished the Bauni for many years, I still cannot advise a fellow angler as to the best time to challenge them. With the *mahseer* of the hills, there seem to be regular feeding times. One of these is at sunset, during what I call the Hour of Gold, as the sun is setting. Perhaps the *mahseer* do not feed at night, so by feeding at this time they try to make sure that they will have something in their stomachs to carry them through the hours of darkness to the following morning. Whatever the reason, I have always found this delightful time of the day, with the dying sun painting the waters gold, and the shadows lengthening, to be the most productive time for a good catch.

The Bauni fish, like most of their brethren everywhere, are carnivorous, and this should be kept mind when choosing instruments with which to collect them. For the most part they eat small fish, so to catch them one either chooses lures that represent small prey, or the actual prey itself. Small fish to use as dead bait can be found in the shallow waters of any WGP stream. But this kind of sitting-and-waiting method of fishing has never appealed to me. For me, the ultimate method is spinning, with a light rod and, for the Bauni fish, a twelve-pound rated nylon line.

For lures, almost anything that will flash and shine in the water is good, though it must always be silver and without attached color. The American Silver Fox lures are good—sizes 4 to 6. The old British spoon bait, originally made by Hardy & Company of Aldwych, England, is often effective, though these days they are very hard to find. And when stocking up on lures, it is good to be aware of the very high rate of attrition that will be imposed by the bottom debris of the Bauni and any of the smaller rivers. One can expect to start the winter season with five dozen lures of all kinds, and to be lucky to finish with any.

Some of the fish that I have taken out of the Bauni over the years, most of them on a catch-and-release basis, are as follows, with the Bauni bridge being used as the demarcation line between the upper and lower sections of the river.

The *Golhai*, (*Notopterus notopterus*). From the upper Bauni, known to the Taru as the *Chattai*. This is a silvery, white fish with a single, small ventral fin and a continuous lateral or lower fin. It may be one of the largest fish of the Bauni. One specimen, caught on a #6 Silver Fox lure, weighed 25lbs. It is also found in the Beri and the Karnali River to an altitude of about 400ft.

The *Rohu*, (*Labeo coeruleus*). From the lower Bauni, a fish of bluish dark coloration, with a yellow tinge. It has fringed lips and a single set of barbels. It is also found in the Kosi area of eastern Nepal.

The *Lalmuha chachara*, (*Ompok bimaculatus*). From the upper Bauni. This is a common catfish, with a laterally compressed body and head. Its coloration varies from silver to grey or even yellow. It has a black spot on the shoulder and sometimes another on the tail.

The *Bohari*, (*Wallago attu*). From the lower Bauni; coloration white with a yellowish tinge along the back and lighter in color below. Sometimes confused with the *Lalmuha chachara*, because it is similar in appearance. However, unlike the *Lalmuha chachara*, its mouth extends back and behind the anterior border of the

The Fishes

eye, while in the other fish it does not. Believed to be a common food of the gharial.

The *Chuche bam*, (*Xenentodon cancila*). From the upper Bauni, in shallow water. In appearance like the marine gar fish, the Chuche bam has long narrow jaws, with the lower jaw protruding beyond the upper. There are many small, sharp teeth set in the jaws; in coloration this fish is green with a white abdomen. The eyes are gold and the body has many small black spots. Has been caught on a one inch silver spoon bait.

The *Hile* or *Chenga*, (*Channa gachua*). Found in the lower Bauni. A fish with four wide gill openings, scales and a depressed head. Oddly, the ventral fin may be either present or absent. The fish is reasonably common in the Terai and ranges into hill streams to an altitude of 4000ft.

The *Bhaura*, (*Channa marulius*). From the upper Bauni. Known to the Taru as the *Ghate*, this fish has a long ventral fin and light red, almost pink, flowerlike markings down either side of the body. These are strangely similar to those found on that most attractive of snakes, the Golden Snake, also known as the Flying Snake. One wonders why nature, in its wisdom, would endow two totally different species, one aquatic and the other terrestrial, with nearly identical camouflage. (See THE SNAKES.)

I have listed eight species that I carefully identified after catching them in the WGP. I have caught some of the other species, but did not list them and so do not have a record. At the same time I have spent many an hour on the upper and lower Bauni under optimum conditions of sunlight and shadow, with the right lures and the best tackle available, and not hooked a single fish.

But, as every true angler knows, ones does not go to a river or a lake to kill fish. One goes to enjoy the day, which for some people simply means getting away from the mundane trivialities of everyday life to spend an hour or two enjoying the beauty and silence of river or lake; to see the flash of a

The White Grass Plains

kingfisher racing past; to hear the heavy wingbeat of a cormorant; to smell the scent of the water as it laps gently on dead logs and rocks; to sit quietly and maybe smile in amusement at the thought of the wily piscatorial inhabitants of the deep, huddled together and shaking their scaly heads in a unanimous vote—Not today my friend, today you're going home fishless. And not caring about that aspect of it one little bit. For the true angler knows that fishing is not really about catching and killing fish. It is something else, something mystic, that only an aficionado of the sport can understand.

The White Grass Plains does not offer the greatest fishing in the world because, as I have already noted, all of the other rivers of the park are too small and too shallow. The Bauni River alone has promise, both in the area of research—the possibility of an unlisted or even unknown species—and for the sport angler. For all in all it is a beautiful river, a true jungle river, and to spend an hour or two at the edge of its dark, slow-moving waters, to the sounds of chattering Rhesus macaques, or the scream of a Fish Eagle, with the wind gently rustling the dark canopy of the trees, and see the little silver minnows, chased by a giant *chattai*, fly like sparks out of the water into the sunlit air, is a truly delightful and privileged experience.

THE WHITE GRASS PLAINS WILDLIFE RESERVE

NEPAL

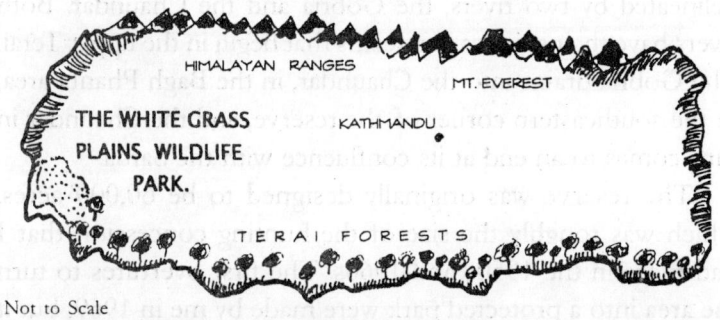

(1) LOCATION AND DIMENSIONS. (2) THE VEGETATION: The forest, grasslands and wetlands. (3) THE RIVERS: The Sarda, the Bauni, the Chaundar, the Gobryia and the Hagania and the small tributaries of each. (4) THE LAKES: Rani Tal, Shikari Tal, Bhatpuri Tal, Kalikitch Tal, Kumari Tal and Sal Gaudi Tal. (5) THE WATERHOLES, NATURAL AND MAN-MADE: Hidden Springs, Nilghai Pokri I, Nilghai Pokri II, Hatti Pokri, Bhaga Tal, Boom Tal and Malu Mela Tal. (6) THE CLIMATE: Summer and winter, forest and plains. (7) ACCESS, BY AIR AND BY ROAD. (8) ENTRY PERMITS. (9) FACILITIES. (10) THE HISTORY OF THE RESERVE, THE

INTERNATIONAL WILDLIFE CONSERVATION SOCIETY, INC, AND THE NEW, WHITE GRASS PLAINS SAFARI LODGE, CONSERVATION AND RESEARCH CENTER.

(1) LOCATION AND DIMENSIONS

The Sukila Phanta Wildlife Reserve is located in the extreme southwest corner of Nepal, in the district of Kanchanpur in the Mahakali zone. Its altitude throughout is about 500 feet above sea level and its land mass drainage slopes gently from north to south. Its northern boundary lies close to the *Bhabar*, which is the gently sloping rise of terrain that lies between the Terai and the towering escarpments of the foothills. Its western boundary and part of its southern boundary is the Sarda River, on the other side of which lies India. Its eastern boundary is delineated by two rivers, the Gobria and the Chaundar. Both rivers have their sources in streams that begin in the upper Terai. The Gobria drains into the Chaundar, in the Bagh Phanta area, in the southeastern corner of the reserve, and the Chaundar in turn comes to an end at its confluence with the Sarda.

The reserve was originally designed to be 60,000 acres, which was roughly the size of the hunting concession that I had there in the 1950s and 1960s. The first overtures to turn the area into a protected park were made by me in 1969, but it was not until 1976 that it was gazetted, or officially registered, as a protected wildlife park. In the interim I spent a full year in the park working to delineate its boundaries, lay out inspection roads and, with a grant from Doris Duke, of New York, NY, built the first bridge on the Bauni River. (The present wooden bridge, tilting alarming and, in 2007, dangerously decayed, is the second; it is now twenty-five years old and is not expected to last much longer.) Later the park was expanded to its present 200,000 acres. Each expansion involved the relocation of many small villages and the problem of finding new land for their people. Eventually, the park was empty of people, a home to wildlife only, which is the way a park should be.

The author confronted by a curious wild elepant in the WGP

The White Grass Plains

The author's daughter, Rara, in the WGP

The White Grass

The author's personal account of big game hunting in north India

The White Grass Plains

The author's story of the great elephant, Tula Hatti

The author's Taru tracker, Narain, of Immelia village

The beauttiful Hidden Springs waterhole, a combined AHF-IWCS project

The Bhaura, (*Channa marulius*) a fish with distinctive markings

The common Langur or Hanuman monkey

The White Grass

The Large-Billed crow that executed the strange, crab-like walk

The man-eating tigress that killed the author's cook

The Russells Viper that the author handled by mistake

The WGP has many species of spider

Through the window of the author's Dodge camper

Toadstools growing in elephant dung

The White Grass

Tree bark, WGP

Tula Hatti, with his huge frontal lobes

Unknown insect in the WGP

Wandering minstrels in a village at the edge of the park

The White Grass Plains

Welding protective pipes on old tube wells

The White Grass

Wild bee hive clusters in the WGP. Left alone they are harmless

Wild bees in a hive containing as many as 100,000 insects

The author's research vehicle in the WGP

Young Asian hyena in the Katmandu zoo. Normally unagressive

(2) THE VEGETATION

The vegetation of the WGP is composed of forest, grasslands and wetlands. The forest is best described as dry tropical and subtropical, consisting mostly of broad-leafed sal (*Shorea robusta*) and sissoo (*Dalbergia sissoo*), interspersed with patches of Khair grass (*Acacia catechu*), better known as elephant grass.

The trees that go to make up the bulk of the existing forest are structured as canopy growth, with an umbrella-like upper growth of mostly large leaves that shade the ground below. This (lack of light) restricts the growth of ground vegetation but at the same time contributes to excellent viewing of wildlife at considerable distances.

Here and there the forest contains patches of elephant grass, some quite small, some of considerable acreage. These thickets, in which the visibility is about three feet, are very dense, with an average growth of about 15ft and single stalks rising to as much as 20ft. They provide excellent habitat for many species of birds, as well as animals like wild boar and Hog deer. They can be penetrated on foot, but not without difficulty. Anyone attempting to do this should give consideration to the possibility of encountering large animals like elephant, which, depending on their mood, may be dangerous, and rhino, which, good mood or bad, are **always** dangerous. There is also the risk of getting lost and the author has experienced this a couple of times.

On both occasions I was out at night, driving off-road, deep in the sal forest, miles from camp and using the stars to guide me. Both times fog came rolling in unexpectedly, blotting out the sky and with it my guiding lights. From experience, I knew it was useless to just keep driving round and round in the ink-black night, trying to find a marker of some kind. So I just bedded down for the night, on the ground, with a little fire to keep warm. On one occasion I was alone; on another, with a terrified client, a lady from Denmark, who was quite sure we were doomed and that our rotting bodies would be found, months hence, 'half eaten by hyenas and other nasties,' as she put it.

Again, more recently, I was temporarily bushed with my daughter Rara when, driving from the Majgaon to Singpur one morning, we left the vehicle to walk to camp, and sent the driver on. We hiked into the forest about two miles north of Singpur, aiming for our Bauni River camp by heading roughly west. It was a bright sunny day and, using the sun as a guide, we made good progress. After about two miles, however, we got into a thick, fifteen-foot high stand of elephant grass in an area known as Sundari Jhal. While we were in it, the sun slipped behind some clouds and when we came out of it, after half an hour of pushing our way through the incredibly thick grass, we found we had lost our direction.

Guessing roughly that we were heading west, and that if we continued on in that direction we would eventually reach the Bauni, we kept going, on a tortuous route. We eventually found the Bauni, about three miles north of our safari camp and followed it down its eastern bank. Finally, the outlines of green canvas tents set under the cool shade of big *sal* trees appeared, welcoming us to drinking water and rest. But the little hike, which should have taken two hours, took seven, and with the shades of night fast falling on the dark halls of the jungle, we were not unhappy to reach camp.

So visitors should keep in mind that **it is possible to get lost** in the WGP if you go off-road, either on foot or in a vehicle. But if this happens, there are ways of regaining direction which are useful to remember. One way is to **try and find a stream or river**, and use it for direction, because all of the streams and rivers of the WGP, with a little wiggle here and there to accommodate elevated ground, basically flow north to south. Another way is to **climb a tree and try to see the foothills**. They lie to the north of the Terai and are a useful direction finder. One should keep in mind, however, that they do not run a true east to west, as many people think, but actually southeast to northwest. A final way, at night, is to **use the stars**. Knowledge of one or two can be very useful, such as the constellation of Cassiopeia—the 'butterfly group'—or Orion's Belt which, with Ursa Major, the so-called Big Dipper, rises out of the east every evening, unfailingly, with the two lower stars of the Dipper aligned directly with the North Star.

The grasslands, or *phantas*, of the WGP, are located in the south central part of the park and consist of an area of about 5000 acres, with scattered islands of trees and some patches of elephant grass. The *phanta* grasses are a beautiful golden brown in color throughout much of the year. In the autumn they produce a white seed, which, as been explained, is what gives the park its Taru name of Sukila Phanta.

Entry by road to the *phantas* from the east is via the Singpur to Balma-Barcola road. (Balma and Barcola were two Taru villages whose people were relocated outside the park during one of its expansions.) From the south, entry is via a ring road that begins on the west bank of the Chaundar River, near the village of Immelia, and travels all along the south side of the *phantas* and the Andaneha. From the north, entry is via the Majgoan to Balma-Barcola road, which begins at the Majgaon guard post and runs down the west side of the park. Within the *phanta*, a single road runs south from the Sukla watchtower, where the village of Sukla used to be, in the north central part of the *phantas*, many years ago. Curling around to the east, it now allows access to a new tower. From there it continues on north, to join the Singpur to Balma-Barcola road, close to the Hidden Springs waterhole.

The park's wetlands, with the exception of the Andaneha, the Great Swamp, can best be described as scattered areas of semi-dry to marshy land, with the water content depending on the season. Typical of these is Kumari Tal, or Kumari Lake, which, during the rains, will contain water to a depth of as much as 2ft, but in the dry season will be completely waterless.

The Andaneha is different, holding its water as it does throughout the year. Its principle water sources are the Hidden Springs waterhole, the Bauni River and, during the rains, some flow-off from the eastern side of the grasslands and the surrounding forest. The Bauni enters the Andaneha in the sal forest not far south of the Singpur to Balma-Barcola road, winds through the impenetrable pattern of its wilderness for several miles and then emerges in the area of the lake known as Shikari Tal.

Within the Andaneha, the average depth of the water will vary from 3–4ft. Underneath this is a soft, muddy bottom into which one can sink to one's thighs, making penetration on foot close to impossible. The author has tried several times to get into the swamp on foot, the last time accompanied by the intrepid explorer Phillip Fry, of Auckland, New Zealand. Each attempt was doomed to failure, partly because of the dense growth, but more because of the combined depth of the water and the mud, bringing our wading depth to a dangerously high chest level. Taru villagers who once lived in the area have told me that no one has ever been into the Great Swamp. They talk of giant snakes—mainly python, of course—and big, seldom-seen tigers.

As tiger habitat, the Andaneha with its deep water and mud does not sound too feasible. But from the heights of a big Strangler fig tree, the author has been able to see small stands of deciduous trees, deep in the tangled mass of brush and elephant grass, suggesting islands of dry land that tigers might use as lairs. Certainly, they would find themselves there in one of the most undisturbed areas of the reserve—something that would appeal to them—and getting in and out of the swamp would not prove too difficult. For tigers are powerful swimmers, as well as which their shape and build would allow them to slip through the dense growth a lot more easily than the physically, vertically-built Byrne and Fry.

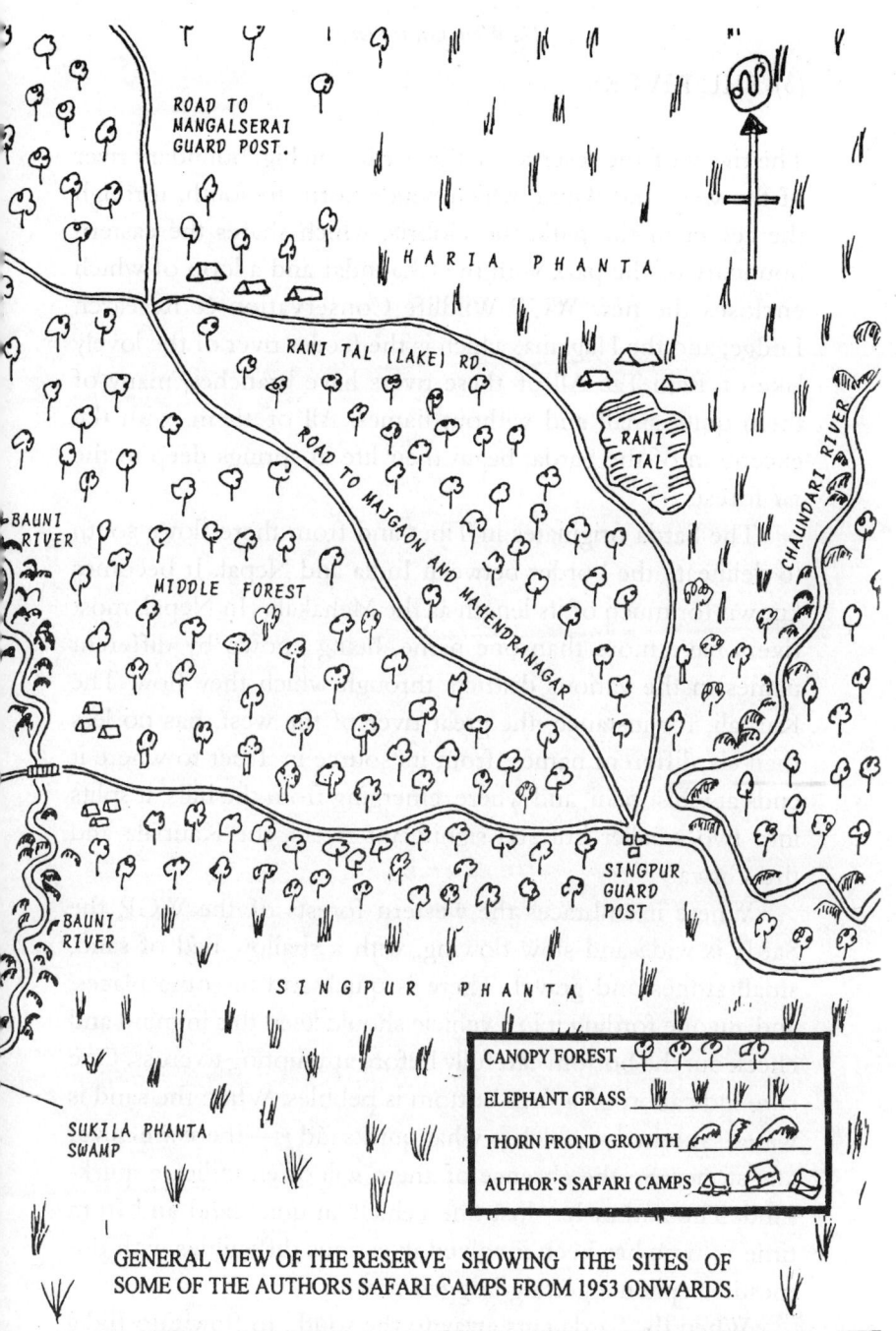

GENERAL VIEW OF THE RESERVE SHOWING THE SITES OF SOME OF THE AUTHORS SAFARI CAMPS FROM 1953 ONWARDS.

(3) THE RIVERS

The rivers of the reserve are the Sarda, the big, boundary river of the west; the Bauni, which winds north to south, through the center of the park; the Gobria, which shares the eastern boundary of the park with the Chaundar and a loop of which encloses the new WGP Wildlife Conservation & Research Lodge; and the Hagania, which is the feeder river of the lovely lake of Rani Tal. All of these rivers have branches, many of them quite small and without names. All of them, with the exception of the Sarda, begin their life in springs deep in the *sal* forests.

The Sarda originates in Tibet and from there flows south to delineate the border between India and Nepal. It becomes known for much of its length as the Mahakali. (In Nepal, most rivers have more than one name, being known by different names in the various districts through which they flow. The Karnali, for instance, the great river of the west, has no less than six different names, from its source in Tibet to where it ends at Chisopani, and where, emerging from the hills, it splits into two smaller but still significant rivers, the Kauriala and the Girwa.)

Where it embraces the western forests of the WGP, the Sarda is wide and slow-flowing, with a shallow bed of sand, small stones and gravel. There is quicksand in some places, and anyone fording it in a vehicle should keep this in mind and check out the bottom carefully before attempting to cross. One sure indication of a firm bottom is pebbles. When the sand is water-saturated—which is what quicksand is—there are never any stones. So the absence of them will often indicate quicksand. The author has lost one vehicle in quicksand and from time to time has been involved in serious difficulties with domestic elephants getting bogged down.

When the Sarda cuts away to the south, to flow into India and become the Gogra, the minimal drop in elevation that

THE AUTHOR'S PROPOSED, 1968 DESIGN FOR THE FIRST BRIDGE OVER THE BAUNI RIVER IN THE W.G.P.

HEIGHT OF BRIDGE ABOVE WATER,	5 feet
WIDTH OF BRIDGE	10 feet
WIDTH OF LOGS TO BE USED	2 feet each
NUMBER OF LOGS ON ROAD SURFACE	5
TOTAL NUMBER OF LOGS	30., 15 to a side, 5 to each deck
EARTH TO BE MOVED	about 20 sq. yards.
NUMBER OF MEN TO BE EMPLOYED	20 to 25
TIME FOR COMPLETION OF EACH BRIDGE	15 to 18 days

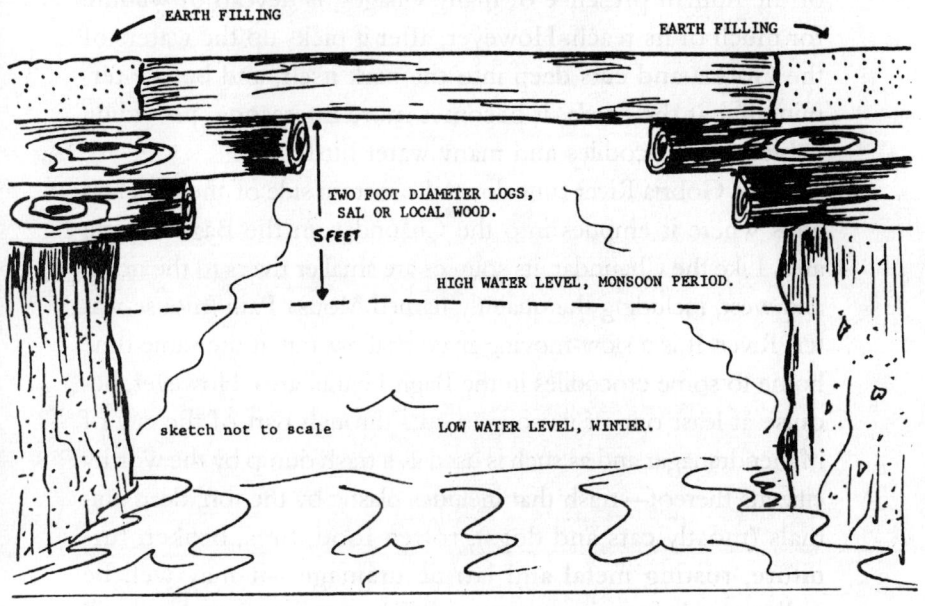

carries it for four hundred miles all the way to the Bay of Bengal, transforms it into a typical, winding, shallow, muddy Indian river, winding snake-like through sand bars and mud flats across the northern plains.

The Chaundar has its origins in a series of smaller tributaries, up in the Bhabar, and from there flows south through the eastern reaches of the park. At one time it fed its waters to Rani Tal and continued on to flow close to the village of Singpur and on again, east and south to its confluence with the Sarda. Then, in the 1960s, during a heavy monsoon, it changed course. Today its old riverbed continues to carry some overflow from Rani Tal. But the river itself now runs a mile or more to the east of the lake, through earthen banks that rise in places to more than 20ft. In its upper reaches, with many villages aligning its eastern bank, it is a pretty river, but, because of the human presence of many villages, is devoid of wildlife for much of its reach. However, after it picks up the waters of the Gobria and cuts deep into the park itself, and before terminating at the Sarda, it becomes more interesting, providing habitat for crocodiles and many water birds.

The Gobria River runs down the eastern side of the park and ends where it empties into the Chaundar, in the Bagh Phanta area. Like the Chaundar, its sources are smaller rivers to the north and west, including the quaintly named Mousa Pani (mouse-water) River. It is a slow-moving river, shallow, but at the same time home to some crocodiles in the Bagh Phanta area. However, because at least one of its sources cuts through part of the city of Mahendranagar and as such is used as a trash dump by the worthy citizens thereof—trash that includes plastic by the ton, dead animals (mostly cats and dogs), rotten food, tires, broken furniture, rusting metal and latrine drainage—it may well be polluted. (A future project of IWCS, funding pending, will be an attempt to clean up this otherwise pretty little river.)

The Hagania begins in springs in the grasslands to the north of Rani Tal, near to where the big Taru village of Haria used to be. Today, with the Chaundar moved away, it is the principal water supply for the lake. For much of its length it is choked with fallen trees and brush and, as of 2007, is dangerously congested. Rivers, like people, can die, and at this time recommendations by the author to have it cleaned out have been ignored. Another IWCS project, funding pending, is to clean the river out, end to end, with an operation similar to that carried out at the beautiful Hidden Springs waterhole. (See 5: WATERHOLES.) The Hagania comes to an end in the still brown waters of Rani Tal.

It is the Bauni that is the true jungle river of the reserve. A slowing-flowing, dark-chocolate colored stream, it weaves its silent way southwards from its sources in springs lying in the north central forests of the reserve. For all of its short, sweet length, it is perhaps less than four miles. Two-thirds of the way down, it enters the impenetrable recesses of the Andaneha, to emerge on the southern side of the great swamp with much of its sediment sieved out by the dense grasses of the interior, much lighter in color, to pour its tea-colored waters into the Chaundar.

The Bauni is home to a great variety of wildlife, from thousands of water-skimmers that live on its surface, to giant python and big tigers with hidden lairs in its upper reaches. It is also alive with fish (see THE FISH) and, unbelievably for such a small river, may contain as many as twenty-seven species, some of them running to as much as 25lbs. A night in a machan on the upper Bauni, with the opportunity to see tiger, rhino and elephant coming down to drink, and maybe a mugger, cold of eye and deadly of purpose, cutting silently through its dark brown waters, is to be taken back in time to a primordial world.

(4) THE LAKES

The largest lake of the reserve, with a surface area of about 1000 acres, is Rani Tal. Many years ago a minor raja, known as the Singpal Raja—a man from the Reu River valley, near

The White Grass Plains

Dandeldura, whose real name was Deuba—had a substantial fort in the forests not far from the lake. It is said that in the evenings his wife, the Rani, would walk to the lake with her ladies-in-waiting, to sit and watch the sun go down and that this is how the lake got its name, Rani Tal, the queen's lake.[5]

The lake is home to a good population of crocodiles and, as of 2007, one *gharial*, the long-nosed saurian that is a fish-eater. The principal habitat of the crocodiles is the lake's northeast corner, where the Hagania River comes in. Swamp deer are seen from time to time, and occasionally elephants. It is home to a fair number of birds but, because of excessive weed growth, not as many as might be expected, in that many species of birds need open water for landing and take-off.

---

[5] Almost nothing is known about the fort of the Singpal Raja. Today the outlines of a huge compound survive, inside the shattered remains of a massive brick wall that was 10ft high and 15ft wide. Outside the wall there was a moat, some 20ft wide and probably, when filled with water, 5ft or 6ft deep. The wall measures more than 1000 yards in circumference and has entryways here and there which were probably gates. Deuba, who built the fort, and thereafter named himself the Singpal Raja, was one of two brothers who came from the Reu River valley, in the hills near Dandeldura. He and his wife were almost certainly there in 1895, because in May of that year a party of young British army officers from the Bareilly cantonment in India came into the area to hunt tiger. One of them, Robert Baden Powell, a man who later became famous for the establishment of the Boy Scouts of the world, kept a diary. One evening that month he wrote in it that it would be nice if the Raja and his Rani, whose fort was close to where they were camped on the Bauni, would invite them to dinner. Soon after that, the Raja and his wife seem to have disappeared and to this day nobody knows, and there appears to be no record, of what happened to them and their retinue. Did they all die of some disease, something like smallpox? Were they attacked, besieged and destroyed by enemies? (Certainly the size of the walls and the presence of a moat suggest that this threat may have existed.) Or did they just leave and move elsewhere, perhaps returning to the Rue River valley, from whence they came in the first place? It is interesting to note that, until now, no large trees have ever grown in the fort's moat, as well as which all traces of buildings within the walled compound have completely disappeared.

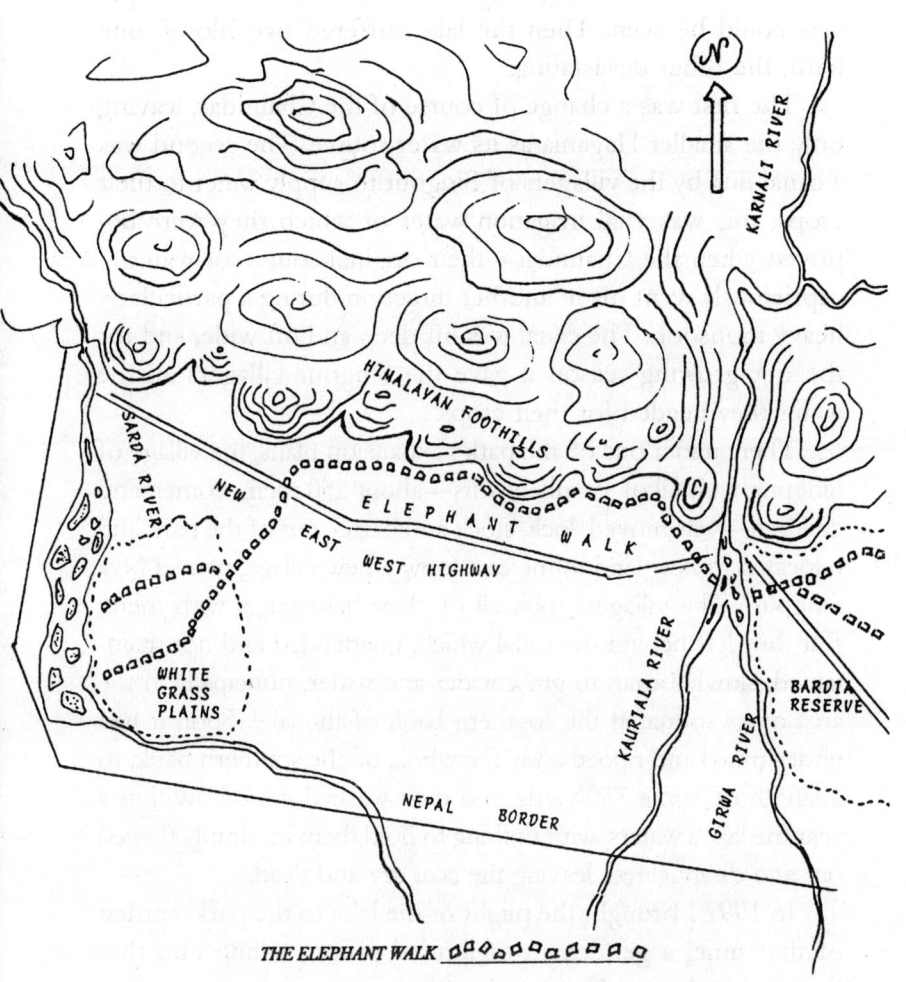

**THE ANCIENT BUT NOW ABANDONED ELEPHANT WALK
BETWEEN THE W.G.P. AND THE BARDIA RESERVE.**

The White Grass Plains

Originally, when the Chaundar River flowed into Rani Tal (See THE RIVERS), and before that river changed its course, the author remembers Rani Tal as having a clear, surface sheet of water where, on any given day, a thousand birds of all species could be seen. Then the lake suffered two blows, one hard, the other devastating.

The first was a change of course of the Chaundar, leaving only the smaller Hagania as its water source. The second was a canal dug by the villagers of Singpur to supply water to their crops; this was vital irrigation water of which they were deprived when the Chaundar—their original source of water—capriciously went off in another direction during a particularly heavy monsoon. The canal was 6ft deep and 6ft wide, and for the rice-growing season it gave the Singpur villagers all the water they needed for their crops.

Then, under one of the park's expansion plans, the village of Singpur, with all of its inhabitants—about 250 men, women and children—was moved, lock, stock and barrel, out of the park and relocated to new land to the east (now a new village, named Nya Singpur.) The villagers took all of their belongings with them. But they left behind the canal which, unattended and not maintained, slowly began to grow wider and wider, principally in the area of its source at the southern bank of the lake. Soon it had undermined and ripped away the whole of the southern bank, to a length of some 750 yards, and then washed it away. Within a year the lake's waters, with nothing to hold them in, simply flowed out and disappeared, leaving the lake dry and dead.

In 1997 I brought the plight of the lake to the park warden of that time, a gentleman of limited vision, telling him that Rani Tal had ceased to exist but that at the same time, with a dedicated project, it could be rehabilitated. As I expected, nothing was done. So I decided to do something on my own and, using the umbrella of IWCS, in a short space of time managed to obtain an adequate grant from the American Himalayan Foundation of San Francisco. Using a local Nepalese

The White Grass

organization known as The Society For The Conservation of Nature and Rural Development, run by a wildlife conservation associate of mine, Hikmat Bisht, of Mahendranagar, the southern bank was completely rebuilt.

With the event of the next monsoon, the lake had refilled, and within weeks, birds by the hundreds had returned, and also fishes. With them, however, and possibly because of the exposure of the lakebed to the torrid summer sun when it was dry, came weeds. Today, two-thirds of the lake's surface is matted and choked with surface growth, which includes lotus and water lilies. Appeals to authorities to apply eradication methods to the problem have produced no response. At this time, various methods are being considered by myself and IWCS, including the possibility of introducing weed-eating carp. Research into this possibility is presently underway and hopefully funding will be available for a weed eradication project when a decision is made to go ahead.

Shikari Tal is a shallow, weed-choked expanse of water lying due south of the Andaneha in the southeast corner of the park, within about a mile of the southern border. Its source of water is the Bauni after it leaves the Andaneha, and it has many fish. The lake is isolated; its northern side has a high bank with a very luxuriant growth of thick, bright green grass and some huge trees. However, because of its proximity to the Indian border, it is subject to poaching from time to time by Indian poachers, using hand nets.

Kumari Tal lies in the central *sal* forests of the park, due east of a marker—a blaze on a roadside tree—that is 1000 yards north of the fourth and most southerly bridge on the Majgoan to Singpur road. Although it is marked on the maps as a lake, it is not a true lake, but is rather a shallow, muddy-bottomed stretch of water, about an acre in extent. In the monsoon it has water to a depth of maybe 2ft. But when winter comes, it dries up completely and stays that way all through the dry months. It has no fish or crocodiles, and few birds.

The White Grass Plains

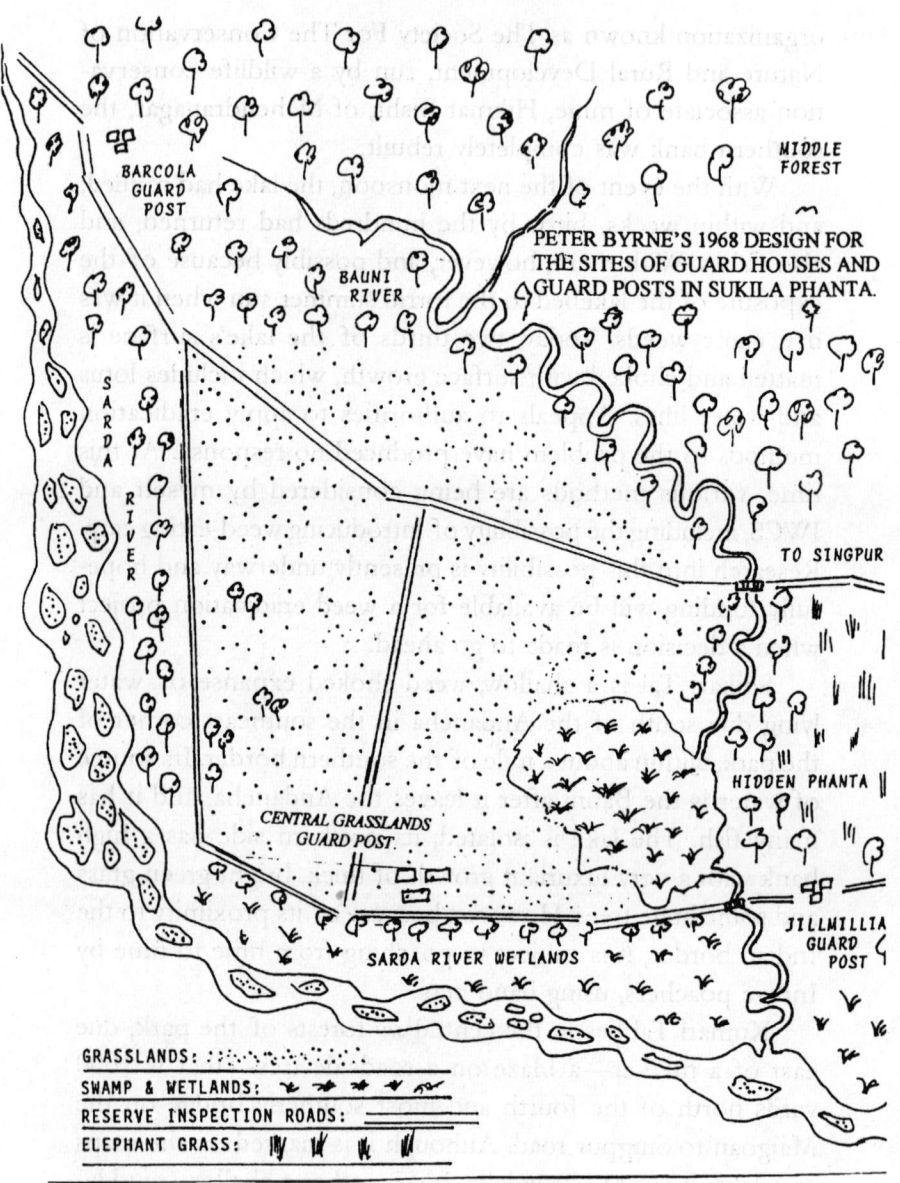

PETER BYRNE'S 1968 DESIGN FOR THE SITES OF GUARD HOUSES AND GUARD POSTS IN SUKILA PHANTA.

The White Grass

Kalikitch Tal is another shallow lake. Like Kumari Tal, it is more of a depression than a lake, holding water only during the rains.

Sal Gaudi Tal is more of a swamp than a lake. Its somewhat romantic name means 'the lake of the throne of the *sal* trees'. It lies in the northeastern sector of the park, about two miles south of Malu Mela, with an access road that runs off the Singpur to Malu Mela road and is also about two miles south of Malu Mela. Years ago it had a fine, clear expanse of water in which crocodiles and many birds could be seen. Its drainage, running out into the Chaundar River, was an open and very attractive marsh, predominated by a pink flower that most delightfully colored its shallow waters. Then suddenly, in the 1990s, the grasses of the main marsh itself, together with the small growths of the drainage, all succumbed to an explosive growth of elephant grass.

Today, though there is a watchtower on the western side of the marsh, little can be seen in the dense, impenetrable 18ft high elephant grass that covers all of the original swamp. Sal Gaudi Tal still has a few crocodiles and is home to three or four rhino, to which its dense cover offers appropriate habitat and security. But the only way to see them would be to wade into the swamp itself, and that is not advisable. A pleasant walk in this area, however, is to hike right around the swamp, starting at the watchtower and going north into the open *sal* forest along the edge of the swamp. From there one would cut due east to pick up the inspection road, just south of Malu Mela. Then the road can be followed, at first south, and then west and then north again, in a circle that goes right around the swamp, back to the tower. On this walk, however, a very careful watch should be kept for rhinos, and an eye for climbable trees in case one is threatened.

This area is one of the few places in the WGP where I have found a rhino dung mound, a hill of droppings 4ft high where one or more rhino practice their peculiar habit of using the same place every day to drop their dung. I am told that they usually do this in the evening, always approaching the mound very cautiously, to make sure there is no danger. Arriving at the mound, they then do something very odd... they turn around and back up to it. Pushing up against the pile until their rear ends are directly above it, they then proceed to defecate on the top. This presumably allows them a comfortable and psychologically satisfactory evacuation. But it also makes them vulnerable to poachers, who remove the huge pile of dung and dig a concealed pit beneath it. When the rhino, backing blindly up to relieve itself, falls in, it is quickly speared to death. The horn is then cut off and taken away and the remainder of the body is left to rot. Rhinos use their dung mounds until these reach a height that makes defecation uncomfortable, then they move on and create another one somewhere else.

(5) THE WATERHOLES

The reserve has a number of waterholes, some natural and some man-made. The man-made holes include Nilghai Pokri I (created by IWCS), Nilghai Pokri II (IWCS), Hatti Pokri (IWCS), Central Phanta Pokri, Upper Phanta Pokri, Bhaga Tal, Boom Tal and Malu Mela Pokri. The single natural waterhole in the park is Hidden Springs, renovated by IWCS in 2002.

Nilghai Pokri I and Nilghai Pokri II, so-named because of the presence of Blue Bull (*nilghai*) antelope in the area, and Hatti Pokri, so named because of an elephant (a *hatti*) that came twice in the night and trampled some of our shovels and metal cement pans, were created by IWCS using grants provided by the American Himalayan Foundation. Each was dug in the winter-dry bed of summer watercourses, shallow rivers that carry monsoonal flow in the summer but are completely waterless for the seven months of the dry season. Using manual labor, with gangs of up to fifty men at a time, the dry courses were excavated to depths that varied from 5–15ft. All brush and dead logs were removed and then each excavation was sealed at its lower end with earth dams surmounted by steel-wire-reinforced concrete spillways, each fortified with flow-absorbing cushions of boulders set against their outer sides. All three waterholes have now (2007) successfully held water for more than six years.

The Central Phanta Pokri is situated in the *phantas* south and west of the central guard post. It is a deep, man-made hole and holds water throughout the year. The Upper *Phanta Pokri* is similar. It is located just north of the central *phanta* guard post, at the site of the one-time village of Sukla. However, possibly because of saturation, it holds less water than the central *phanta* hole. At about the time it was dug, however, probably noticing this loss of water, the resident warden, a gentleman afflicted with perennial myopia, decided that it might be useful to run a feeder channel from the Bauni River down to the new hole and he had one dug. Fortunately, his incredibly stupid and ill-thought plan was discovered in time and the channel was blocked off and closed. What this would have done to the Andaneha, for which the Bauni is the main source of water, does not bear thinking about. The channel itself, which would almost certainly have been left unattended, might well in time have altered the very course of the Bauni itself.

Boom Tal and Malu Mela Tal are also man-made, again by park authorities. Both are ground-water holes and, because of this, successfully hold water throughout the year to a depth of about 3ft. Boom Tal, with a name that is sinister in origin, lies on the east side of the Majgaon to Singpur road, about 1½ miles south of the Majgaon army guard post. Malu Mela Tal lies to the west of the branch road that runs (roughly parallel-ing the main Singpur to Majgaon road) from Malu Mela, north to Majgaon; it is located about 1 mile north of Malu Mela.

Bhaga Tal (Tiger Lake) lies east of the main Majgaon to Singpur road about 3 miles south of Majgaon. It has a wooden watchtower for wildlife observation. It is spring-fed and holds some water throughout the year. In recent years a park warden has enlarged it and renamed it Baba Tal after one of his children. However, the original name is the one by which the Tarus know it, and have always known it, and hopefully in time the childish renaming of it will be forgotten.

The Hidden Springs waterhole lies in the northeastern sector of the *phantas* close to the Y junction of the Singpur to Balma-Barcola road, where this road enters the *phantas* proper. It is set in a fine stand of old trees, which shade its waters. It is oblong in shape, the configuration being west to east, and is about 1000ft in length and 20ft wide. Its powerful spring, which has no equal in the park, is situated at its western end. Its waters are clear and cold; they bubble up from deep in the earth to flow smoothly and gently eastwards through its long, narrow pool, into the Andaneha. The pool has small fish, and otters come to it from time to time. It is a quiet and beautiful place, a place for meditation and contemplation, and its southern bank makes for a delightful, temporary campsite.

In 1993, reading the ground signs there, I noticed that very few animals— and no small animals, like young deer—were coming to drink at the hole. The reason was obvious; it was jammed with debris—mostly fallen and rotting trees and brush—from end to end, a massed barrier of twisted branches and decaying tree trunks that effectively prevented most animals from getting to the water. Through IWCS, and with a grant from the American Himalayan Foundation, I undertook the work of cleaning out the hole. The operation employed thirty men and took three weeks, during the course of which I had a very risky encounter with a Russell's Viper (see SNAKES). When we had finished the cleanup and the saturated debris we had taken out of the hole was dry enough, we stacked and burned it. We then cut four gently sloping dirt ramps down through the banks, to allow animals to reach the water to drink, and concluded the work by cutting a small trail right around

The White Grass

the hole. Today many animals, including tiger, come to Hidden Springs to drink, and it is a delightful place to visit.

(6) THE CLIMATE

The WGP has essentially two seasons—summer and winter. The change between them takes place in a matter of days and, as Corbett noted, is so subtle that spring and autumn are virtually unknown. The winter season, which I call the north Indian winter, is generally regarded as being the months of November, December, January and February. In these months there are two ranges of temperature, one for the forest and one for open areas, like the *phantas*. In the forest, winter day temperatures range in the 70°Fs, and nights in the 50°Fs. In open country it is cooler, with day temps in the 60°Fs and nights generally ranging in the 40°Fs, with a fast drop of temperature through the afternoons and pre-dawn cold snaps that will plunge the thermometer to a frosty 30°F. When camping in the park in the winter, it is advisable to keep in mind the very sharp drop in temperature that begins in the late afternoon. It can be as much as thirty degrees, and to be caught in the open without protective clothing, though not life-threatening, can be chillingly uncomfortable.

Winter humidity in both open country and forest is high, bringing dense morning fog that in January and February may sometimes hang in all day, with the sun nothing more than a weak yellow orb unhappily glimmering behind the thick grey blanket. If one is camping, this can mean soaked tents and damp camp equipment, for days. However, this heavy dewfall is essential to the vegetation; without it, for the nearly seven months of the dry season, just about all the plant life of the Terai would perish.

Summer weather conditions in the WGP are quite the opposite of winter. The summer heat begins to build in April, with temperatures growing through this month into the 80°Fs and 90°Fs. Part of the reason for this is the Loo, an infamous and perennial wind that comes roaring up from the deserts of Rajasthan, in north India, with blasts of hot air that are nothing less than fiery gusts from the mouth of hell. The wind carries a grey, sandy dust from the deserts that creates depressingly leaden skies.

April then merges into May, which is the hottest month of the year in the Terai, with scorching temperatures up to as much as 115°F in the afternoons. In June the monsoon comes and the pitiless temperatures drop a bit. But they stay over 100°F in the day and not much less at night, right through to mid-October. Then the rains come to an end and, within the last two weeks of October, in western Nepal, cool, Indian Ocean air starts flowing up from the southwest, heralding the arrival of another delightful winter.

May is a dry month, but might have pre-monsoon storms, with short bursts of heavy rainfall and much thunder and lightening. The monsoon itself brings great tropical storms, with earth-shaking thunder, vivid lightning and a precipitation of hundreds of inches. After it settles in, in July, the monsoon rains seem to fall mostly at night and into the early morning. Why this is, I do not know. I do know that at times it is so heavy that windshield wipers on a vehicle cannot cope with it and, if driving, one may be forced to pull over and wait for it to stop.

Finally, the WGP has two peculiarities of winter weather that are quite fascinating. One, that the Tarus call the *chota bersathi*, or the little monsoon, seems to defy explanation. It is a three-day period of rain, wind and sometimes thunder and lightning—a cold tropical storm—that occurs, completely out of place, so to speak, in the middle of the winter, the dry season. Why this happens, I do not know, and to date I have not been able to find a meteorologist who could explain it to me. It usually comes in December or early January, and I and winter visitor friends have had more than one Christmas camp drenched in its torrential, pounding, cold rain.

The other interesting oddity of the Terai weather is the dawn wind. Dawn in the Terai—to me the most beautiful part of the day—begins with a thin, pale band of color in the east, sometimes nothing more than a faint glow. As one watches, this thin light fades and disappears; what one has seen is called the false dawn. Within minutes, the true dawn begins to color the eastern horizon, seizing the dark blue skies of night and painting them in shades of violet and gold. As it does, for a period of about five minutes, no more, and sometimes even less, a fairy-light wind arises to dance through the dry grass of the forest floor, gently rustling the stems, and here and there softly turning over a brown leaf. It is so light, it is barely perceptible. It is also close to silent and, from the inside of a tent, if one is not listening for it, it will hardly be heard. Five minutes, maybe four, and then, as mysteriously as it arises, it disappears and is gone. As it dies, the dawn light begins to grow, to bathe the forest in pale shades of blue and gold. It is soon followed by the yellow winter sun, climbing fast out of the east to soar over the forest and thrust great shafts of light down through the canopy of the trees—sunbeams like swords heralding another glorious Terai winter day.

(7) ACCESS TO THE WGP, BY AIR AND ROAD

Access to the WGP begins, for most people, in Katmandu, from where there are two methods of reaching the far west and the reserve. One is by road, by private car. The distance to Mahendranagar—the city that lies closest to the reserve—from Katmandu is 420 miles. Whereas this is something one can happily drive in 8 hours in most western countries, in Nepal the pace, set as it is by highway 'obstacles' in the form of wildly-driven trucks and buses, pedestrians and cyclists, buffaloes, cows, goats, pigs, sheep, horses and dogs is, shall we say, a trifle slower. So, if going by car, it is best to plan a two-day trip. A city that is roughly halfway between Katmandu and Mahendranagar is Butwal. It has a few hotels, including a pleasant one called the Sindoor, where one can spend a comfortable night and get a reasonably decent meal.

The second mode of transport is to go by bus. I have never been on a bus, so cannot speak from experience. But I have been told that it is something of a hair-raising experience and, in addition, a grueling, 18-hour, non-stop run. Buses leave Katmandu at about midday, so much of the travel is at night. It is also now possible to get a 'deluxe' bus in the morning from Katmandu to the Indian border at Sonauli, getting off en route at Butwal. This will shorten the discomfort of the journey somewhat, though not entirely, as the rest of the journey will have to be done on a local bus!

The best way to get to the west is obviously by air. The western airfields are now served by a number of airlines, among them Buddha, Sita and Nepal Airlines. At one time Mahendranagar had an airfield, which was very convenient for people visiting the WGP, being situated within a bare 300 yards of the park entrance. It is still there, but has been closed for many years. Now one flies to a border city called Nepalgunj, from where it is possible to reach the reserve, by car, in about 5 hours. Or better still, to Dhangari, another border city, from where it is a 1½ hour drive to both the WGP and, as of 2007, to the IWCS safari lodge that is the author's conservation and research center.

Airline ticketing in Katmandu is best done through a travel agency. An efficient one with pleasant staff, which I and friends have used for years, is Sun Kosi Travel, of Katmandu, it's somewhat unfortunately named website and email address being www.sunkoshitours.com and sunkoshitt@wlink.com.np. Their telephone number in Katmandu is (00 977 1) 5548067, via which one can make a booking by phone and have the ticket brought to a hotel. The cost of a round-trip flight, Katmandu–Mahendranagar is, for Nepalese citizens, $165, but, for foreigners, $350.00, which must be paid in foreign currency.

(8) WGP ENTRY PERMITS, CAMPING, ETC.

The headquarters of the park are at a place called Majgaon, about 3 miles from the center of Mahendranagar. Majgaon has a substantial army post, from where platoons of soldiers patrol the park, usually on bicycles. Entry permits to the park, for day visits and for camping, are issued at the park headquarters. The present fee for a foreigner to spend a day in the park is Rs.500, which is about $7.50, depending on the current rate of exchange. The daily fee for taking a car into the park is Rs.2000, or about $30.00. The fee for camping (overnight) is Rs.1000, or about $15.00. The fee for rent-an-elephant, if one is available, is Rs.500 or about $7.50 per day, and fishing licenses costs Rs.500 or about $7.50 per day.

Park authorities may insist on visitors taking a guide into the park; sometimes one is available, sometimes not. Walking in the park is allowed, but is not advisable. One way to see the park is by bicycle—a round trip though the park means riding about 25 miles. A sign at the entrance to the park states that it is closed from sunset to sunrise. It also states that no drinking of alcoholic beverages is allowed within the reserve. But at the Shikari Sahib bar, in my Bauni River camps, I and my friends have unanimously resolved that it is an accepted fact that some rules were made to be broken.

(9) FACILITIES

There are no facilities for visitor accommodation either in the park or anywhere near it. None! There was a small lodge situated at the main entrance, years ago, called the Burra Singha Lodge. It was, shall we say, somewhat diminutive, with a total of two rooms renting at about $2 a night per person, and dinner—rice and lentils—for about another $1. But the park, as it has always been, was just too far off the beaten track for visitors and its owners soon went out of business.

The White Grass Plains

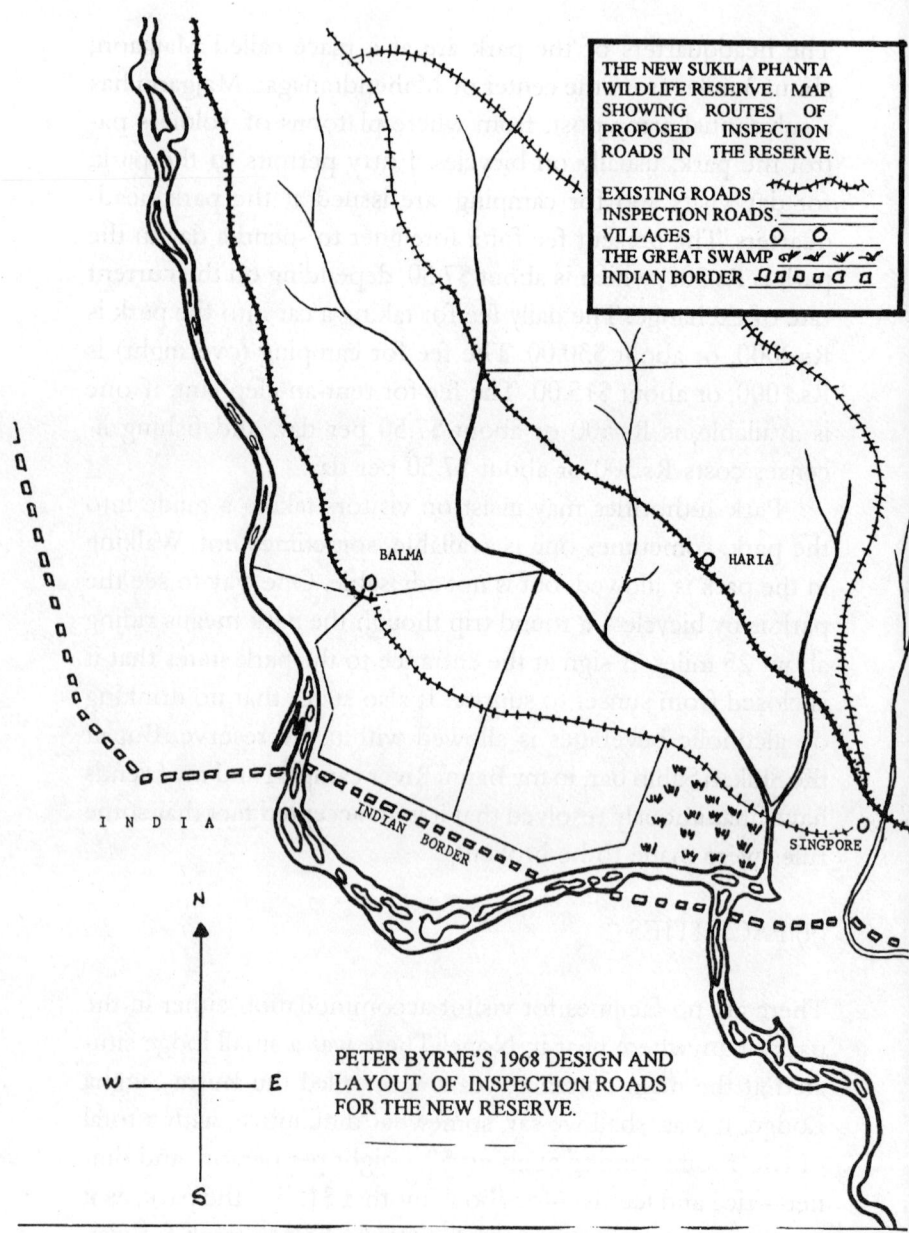

PETER BYRNE'S 1968 DESIGN AND LAYOUT OF INSPECTION ROADS FOR THE NEW RESERVE.

Mahendranagar, 3 miles from the park's main gate, has a 14-room hotel rather quaintly named the Sweet Dream, with accommodation from $5–15 per night per person, a dining room with plain meals served at a not-to-be-hurried pace, and pleasant and courteous staff. It lies on the main east-west highway at the eastern edge of the city.

(10) THE HISTORY OF THE PARK, THE INTERNATIONAL WILDLIFE CONSERVATION SOCIETY, THE NEW WHITE GRASS PLAINS SAFARI LODGE, CONSERVATION AND RESEARCH CENTER

In 1968, after 18 years as a professional hunter, preceded by five years as an amateur big game hunter while I was a tea planter in north Bengal, I decided to give up big game hunting and turn to conservation. There were several reasons. One was the obvious decline of wildlife in India. Another was the sickening slaughter of tigers by the Indian professional hunting companies (one of which proudly boasted of having killed 800 tigers!) Another was the great respect that I had developed for all kinds of wildlife over the years, something that probably went back to my boyhood years among the lakes and forests of southern Ireland and what my father had taught me about respecting nature. That was a long time ago. But I feel it undoubtedly contributed to and was now part of a new reluctance to be involved in any more killing. Another was the realization that, if I did give up hunting and turn to conservation, at the same time establishing some kind of professional wildlife protection program, I could actually continue living the same kind of life which I had enjoyed so much until then, which included spending eight months of every year under canvas in the magnificent forests of the Terai.

Armed with my ideas and a written proposal, I went to Katmandu and sat down with a Mr. Ram Bahadur Thapa, Chief Conservator of the Department of Forests. He was a man with

The White Grass Plains

whom I had already had some dealings in connection with hunting licenses, and the person who would make any decisions towards what I wanted, in that there was no wildlife or conservation department in Nepal at that time. My proposal was simple; take back my hunting concession in west Nepal and turn it into a protected park. I added that, as in my opinion Sukila Phanta, the WGP, was still one of the most pristine and unspoiled areas of the Nepal Terai at that time, it truly deserved to be protected for the future.

Mr. Thapa was interested and said that he thought my proposal to be a very good one. He promised his support. But alas, he said, the department had no funds for anything like that just then, and if I wanted to have a shot at doing it, I would have to find the funding myself. I believe that it was somewhat to Mr. Thapa's surprise when I said that I would do just that, and also that I would start at once to try and find the money needed.

A few days later I left Katmandu and flew to Europe. My plan was to approach the major conservation institutions of the world and get them to contribute to the creation of a new reserve in Nepal. The theme that I would use would be based on what I believed about tigers, which was that mainly because of their slaughter in India, they were now seriously endangered.

I started with the I.U.C.N., the International Union For The Conservation of Nature, probably the most influential conservation establishment in the world at this time and based in Morges, Switzerland. Arriving in Morges, I bunked up at a small hostel and started a round of the various I.U.C.N offices, And I have to say, even now, after all these years, that I was shocked at the reception that I received. It was, essentially, go away, we don't want to talk to you. We don't know you—we've never heard of you. You don't belong to any organization? You are what, a field man? An ex-professional hunter? As for tigers being endangered, the notion is ridiculous.

The White Grass

If they were, they said, raising their eyebrows and looking down their noses at me, we would know about it and they would be listed in our Red Book of endangered species. They are not listed. Therefore they are not endangered. You don't know what you are talking about. End of argument. Go away.

I found the attitude of the Swiss both rude and offensive, as have many others in the world of wildlife conservation. After a fruitless week of failing to get anyone to pay attention to my project—forget about getting any of their precious conservation money—I left Morges and flew to London.

In London I approached the World Wildlife Fund and, while I was treated there with a little more courtesy than in Switzerland, the answer was much the same. No money for a protected park in faraway Nepal and certainly no money for tigers; why, they were not in the Swiss Red Book and therefore they could not possibly be endangered.

Leaving London, I flew to the US and in Washington DC approached an acquaintance—a man who was later to become a firm friend—a Mr. Leonard Fink, an attorney in general practice. Skip, as he was known to his friends, and his gracious wife, Amelia, put me up at their delightful house in Georgetown. Skip sat down with me to try and find a way to help me in my quest. What we needed, Skip reasoned, was a funding entity of some kind through which we could attract potential donors and, through them, raise money for the project. The very best vehicle, he thought, would be a not-for-profit foundation or society, with a not-for-profit tax status which would allow donors various degrees of tax benefits.

With introductions from Skip, and through him from others, we put together a team consisting of two brilliant Washington DC surgeons and another attorney. The surgeons were Karl Jonas and Lyman Sexton and the additional attorney was the colorful and well-known Scott Whitney. All of them contributed much of their valuable time via a number of dinners and luncheons, at all of which I gave talks about my background, the project, and what I hoped for the future of the WGP. Skip himself, without fees of any kind, did all of the legal paperwork necessary for the establishment and registration, with 501 (c) 3 tax status, of the International Wildlife Conservation Society Inc.

Three months later, armed with the imposing title of Executive Director of the new society, and with a healthy purse, I returned to Nepal and set about the work of establishing the new reserve. I camped in the park for twelve months, right through the monsoon rains, with breaks only to go back and forth to and from Katmandu to confer with Ram Bahadur Thapa and his assistant, Assistant Chief Conservator Emerald Jung Rana. (There were no air services operating in Nepal at this time and no roads from the west to Katmandu, so trips had to be by road through India, each one a rough, round-trip journey of six days.)

I trained game scouts in the work of animal counting, identification and recording, had uniforms made for them, gave them bicycles, water bottles, sun hats, compasses, binoculars and rain gear and, working with local villagers—many of whom still lived in the park at this time—demarcated the park, mapped it and put in inspection roads. By mid-1969 the work was concluded, and in early summer I pulled out and went down to Australia for six months to visit my parents, who had moved there from Ireland.

When I came back, I opened up a photo safari operation in the far west. Still later I founded one of the first whitewater rafting companies in Nepal. These commercial operations were necessary, for the end of big game hunting meant for me the end of a very healthy income and with IWCS I had made it clear to all concerned that I would always work as a non-paid volunteer, which I have done to this day.

While running my photo safaris and my rafting company, I kept IWCS active and registered and at least once a year, as time allowed, used it to operate at least one preservation project in the park. Again, with personal experience of what can happen to conservation funding in Asia, especially how it can be dissipated down what is cynically known as the Great Asian Rat Hole, I made a resolution that the society would always keep all of its programs within a single area, the area which gave rise to the birth of the society in the first place, the White Grass Plains.

To this day, this policy has been maintained and now, in 2007, a dream of the society, and of mine, is about to come true with the establishment of the new White Grass Plains Safari Lodge Conservation and Research Center. The new center is being built on purchased private land just off the southeastern side of the park, close to its boundary. The name of the area is Bagh Phanta, which means the Plain Of The Tigers and it lies just five miles south of the junction of its access road with the main east-west highway from Katmandu to Mahendranagar. The site of the lodge covers eleven acres and its boundary is a big loop of the Gobria, a jungle river where wild elephant and tiger come to drink and where big muggers sun themselves on its sandy banks. .

The safari lodge was originally planned as a not-for-profit lodge that would entertain tourists on a commercial basis, but with all net profits being directed into conservation programs in the park. Then, during the time it took to raise the funding, I have to admit that I had a change of heart about entertaining guests—which essentially meant tourists, albeit high-paying ones. I just felt that I had done enough of that throughout my hunting years, then after that with my photo safaris and again with my commercial river trips. So I abandoned that approach and looked at another one.

Careful consideration of what would be best for the park convinced me that a much better idea would be to make the lodge a scientific center, one that would act as a base for academics carrying out research programs in the WGP. Nominal fees for their board and lodging, with access to all the research facilities of the center, would sustain the cost of running the lodge with, once again, as in the original plan, net profit, if any, to be channeled into local conservation projects. In addition to visiting scientists, the center would also offer accommodation and facilities for students involved in advanced studies in disciplines related to the eco-systems and bio-diversity of the park. This plan, I felt, would in the long run be much more beneficial to the reserve than the tourist option. So this is the plan that I and IWCS have adopted.

With the publication of this little book the new safari lodge and research center should be up and running, with researchers in place and conducting projects beneficial and meaningful to the park. The construction should all be finished—it will have taken two years—and the lodge will be operating as a scientific center, a base for dedicated research in the WGP.

Apart from that, it will be something else. It will be a place which people who have supported and contributed to its founding, as well as the author's personal friends, can come to visit. To spend time in the park on elephant back, or in a 4X4 vehicle, or in the beautiful grounds of the lodge itself. To sit at its big river-stone fireplace with a roaring log fire fighting off the chill of the winter evening and at the same time savor the aromas of good food cooking in the kitchen. To relax outside on the big, shaded front porch, to watch the sun sink into the dark treeline of the WGP.

Or sit at the Shikari Sahib bar, to exchange reminiscences of field and stream with other friends, perhaps even with the old pukka sahib in residence. And maybe have him explain what the safari lodge, and its purpose, really mean to him, which is the joy, at long last, of being able to give something back to a place which, for so many years, has enhanced his life and, in the process, given him so much pleasure.

GLOSSARY

A
ASL – above sea level

B
baboo or babu – an Indian clerk in government or private service
bagh – tiger
Bagh Phanta – The Plain Of The Tigers, adjacent to the WGP
Bagha Tal –Tiger Lake. Actually a waterhole of this name in the WGP
ban – forest
ban mahola – king, or kings, of the forest. (Native name for the Red Dog)
barbel (s) – spines or whiskers on fish; common to catfish
beam – in deer, the principal vertical stem, or trunk, of the horns
Bhabar – the gently sloping land between the Terai and the foothills
Burrumpooter – the old colonial name for the Brahmaputra River

C
cantonment – British military compound during the days of the Raj
carapace – bony, body-enclosing shell of a turtle or tortoise
carnivorous – meat-eating
Catmandoo – the original spelling of Katmandu
caudal – of the tail (of a reptile)
cheetal – the Axis Deer. Also known as the Spotted Deer
chitua – leopard; also sometimes called a chota bagh, i.e. a small tiger

coolie – old and quite respectful British Indian name for a porter
Corbett – James (Jim) Corbett, the legendary, India-domiciled, man-eater hunter of Irish ancestry
crepuscular – active (in movement) in the late evening or early morning

D
diurnal – daytime, daylight hours
dudee – thicket, usually of elephant grass

F
feringhee – foreigner

G
gaff – steel hook with a wooden handle used to lift fish out of the water.
gaira - wet, or marshy, or muddy area
gharial – the long-nosed, fishing-eating crocodile of the Terai
goo – tiger and other animal droppings

H
hatti – elephant
herbivorous – feeding on only vegetable matter
hibernation – complete or sometimes partial winter torpor
Hindoo, or *Hindu* – an Indian of the Hindu faith
Hindoostan – historical name for India
Hindustani – the common language of India, now more commonly called *Hindi*

J
jungle – a word in Hindustani meaning roughly any kind of forest or brush

K
keel – elongated ridge (of scales) of a snake
khat – timber

Glossary

khet or *khetti* – land on which rice is grown
khola – river or stream

L

laguna – Hog deer, one of the smaller deer species of the WGP grasslands
lateral – lower, relating to fish; as in a lateral or lower fin

M

Madesh – name for the country of India used among villagers in Nepal
Madeshi – ethnic group of people who live in the Indo-Nepal border area, known as the Terai
maidan – a grassy open space, a field, or a park, or playing field
mandir or *mandu* – a temple
maund – a measure of weight, about 82lbs
mugger – the broad-nosed, carnivorous crocodile of the Terai
musth – in elephants, a period of heightened sexual activity, mostly in males, and lasting from four to six weeks, at least once a year

N

Nepaul – old British spelling of Nepal
nocturnal – of the hours of darkness, the night
nuchal – area of the back of the neck
nuddie – minor river or stream
nullah – ravine or ditch

O

olfactory – sense of smell
omnivorous – living on food that will include animal and vegetable matter
ovoviviparous – creating eggs that hatch within the uterus

P

padi or *paddy* – young rice plants
Paharia – Nepalese people who live in the hills

pedicels – in deer, the bony root structure from which the horn grows
peepul – a species of large tree sacred to Hindus
phalanges – digit bones of a snake
phanta – a plain, or flat
plantigrade – locomotion on the soles of the feet
pokri – a large pond
Prater – author of the 'bible' of Indian zoologists, see BIBLIOGRAPHY
pukka – from the days of the Raj, meaning proper, upright, gentlemanly

R
Raj – the name given to the period of British colonialism in India
reserve – an old British Indian term for government-owned land

S
safari – a Swahili word meaning a journey, but more often used to describe a hunt
sal – common hardwood of the Terai (Shorea robusta)
seall – jackal
seer – measure of weight, about two pounds. Also Hindi for a tiger
shikar – to hunt
shikari – hunter but also, according to Hobson Jobson, a gentleman
soo soo – Gangetic or Pink dolphin of the lower Himalayan and Terai rivers
sounder – a group of family of wild boar, or Pigmy hog
spoon bait – old time fishing lure made by Hardy & Co, Aldwych, England
strangler fig – a large species of parasitic tree
sundar – beautiful
Sundarban – forests and waterways of the Brahmaputra River delta. Also known as the Sundarbans

Glossary

T

tal – a lake, or large pond
Taru or *Tharu* – the indigenous people of the Terai
Dangora Taru – one of the clans, or tribes, of the Taru people
Rana Taru – one of the clans or tribes of the Taru people
tine – in deer, a stem or branch of the horns
Terai – the gently rising stretch of land that runs all across southern Nepal from the edge of the plains, north, to the edge of the Bhabar; much of it is forested and is home to the Taru people

V

ventral – upper, relating to fish; as in a ventral or upper fin
viviparous – producing live young

BIBLIOGRAPHY

Champion, Frederick Walker. WITH A CAMERA IN TIGERLAND, Doubleday, New York, 1928. THE JUNGLE IN SUNLIGHT AND SHADOW, Chatto & Windus, London, 1934.
Burke, W. S. THE INDIAN FIELD SHIKAR BOOK, The Indian Field Office, Calcutta, 1908.
Gee, E.P. THE WILDLIFE OF INDIA, Collins, London, 1964.
Sanderson, Ivan T. LIVING MAMMALS OF THE WORLD, Hamish Hamilton, London, 1955.
Ali, Salim. INDIAN HILL BIRDS, Oxford University Press, Delhi, 1949.
Baden-Powell, Sir Robert. INDIAN MEMORIES, Herbert Jenkins, London, 1915.
Corbett, Jim. MAN-EATERS OF KUMAON, THE MAN-EATING LEOPARD OF RUDRAPRAYAG, THE TEMPLE TIGER AND OTHER MAN-EATERS, JUNGLE LORE, MY INDIA. Oxford University Press, New York and London, 1944 and onwards. Safari Press, Huntington Beach, CA, a very fine, collectors, slip-covered, limited edition, 2002.
Daniel, J.C. THE BOOK OF INDIAN REPTILES, Bombay Natural History Society and Oxford University Press, 1983.
Grimmett, Richard and Inskipp, Tim and Carol. BIRDS OF NEPAL, Delhi, India, Prakash Books, 2000. And, BIRDS OF THE INDIAN SUB CONTINENT, Christopher Helm, London, England, 1998.

Bibliography

Inglis, the Honorable James, M.L.A. TENT LIFE IN TIGER LAND AND SPORT AND WORK ON THE NEPAUL FRONTIER, Sampson Low, Marston & Company Ltd, London, 1892.

Mountfort, Guy. SO SMALL A WORLD, Hutchinson, London, 1974.

Prater, S.H., C.M.Z.S. THE BOOK OF INDIAN ANIMALS, The Bombay Natural History Society and Oxford University Press, 1848.

Sterndale, R.A. SEONEE; CAMP LIFE ON THE SATPURA RANGE, Thacker Spink & Co, Calcutta, India, 1887.

Symington, John, M.D. IN A BENGAL JUNGLE, Chapel Hill, University of North Carolina, 1955.

Turner, J.E. Carrington. MAN-EATERS AND MEMORIES. Robert Hale Ltd, London, 1959.

Williams, J.W. ELEPHANT BILL, Country Life Press, New York, 1950.

Woodcock, Martin. BIRDS OF THE INDIAN SUBCONTINENT, William Collins & Son, London, 1980.

Wright, Belinda and Stanley Breedon. THROUGH A TIGER'S EYES; A CHRONICLE OF INDIAN'S WILDLIFE, Berkley, Ten Speed Press, 1996.

Yule, Henry and A.C. Burnell. HOBSON-JOBSON, THE ANGLO INDIAN DICTIONARY, Wordsworth Editions Ltd, Hertfordshire, UK, 1996. Originally published by Wordsworth Reference, 1886.

MacDonald, A. St. J. CIRCUMVENTING THE MAHSEER IN INDIA AND BURMA, Bombay Natural History Society, Bombay, India, c. 1948.

Byrne, Peter. TULA HATTI, THE LAST GREAT ELEPHANT, Faber & Faber, Manchester, NH, 1995. GONE ARE THE DAYS, 2000 and GENTLEMAN HUNTER, 2007, both by Safari Press, Huntington Beach, California, USA.

REFERENCE BOOKS USED BY THE AUTHOR

Baden Powell, Sir Robert. INDIAN MEMORIES.
Blandford, W. T. THE FAUNA OF BRITISH INDIA, MAMMALIA.
British Museum, GAME ANIMALS OF INDIA.
Burke, W.S. THE INDIAN FIELD SHIKAR BOOK.
Champion, F.W. THE JUNGLE IN SUNLIGHT AND SHADOW.
Champion, F.W. WITH A CAMERA IN TIGERLAND.
Daniel, J.C. THE BOOK OF INDIAN REPTILES.
Dunbar Brander, A.A. WILD ANIMALS IN CENTRAL INDIA.
Jerdon, T.C. THE MAMMALS OF INDIA.
Lydekker, R. THE GREAT AND SMALL GAME OF INDIA.
Pocock, R.I. THE FAUNA OF BRITISH INDIA, MAMMALIA.
Prater, S. H., C.M.Z.S. THE BOOK OF INDIAN ANIMALS.
Shrestha, Dr. Jivan. FISHES, FISHING IMPLEMENTS & METHODS OF NEPAL.
Stewart, A.E. TIGER AND OTHER GAME.

ACKNOWLEDGEMENTS

I am indebted to a large number of people whose support in many and various ways has contributed to the writing of this little book, from humble Taru villagers of the Nepal Terai, to sophisticates of the great cities of the world. Here I will list those that come to mind, asking forgiveness of anyone, who, through simple absentmindedness on my part, may not be included.

Cathy Griffin, my partner of a decade, for roughing it uncomplainingly on safari with me in Terai forest and jungle river and for her loving and unstinting support of my many projects, good and bad, successful and unsuccessful, hilarious and the opposite, through the years.

My dear daughter Rara, for her encouragement of this work, her companionship on safari and her great interest in the jungle folk of the Terai forests—all things great and small—including but not limited to her careful identification of the Common Krait she dug out of a riverbank during our rafting run—a first descent—of the western Rapti River.

Bill, Beryl and Michael Green, for perennial encouragement of my writing. Phillip Fry, of Auckland, New Zealand, for his in-the-field contributions, not the least of which was a valiant attempt to penetrate the Andaneha, the Great Swamp.

The very generous people whose support has sustained the International Wildlife Conservation Society through the years, which institute in turn has helped to preserve the White Grass Plains, the scene and background of this book, including (but not limited to) Karen Gough of Miami, Florida, Holly Hines of Atlanta, Georgia, Tom Dadras of Los Angeles, Eric Tablada of Marina Del Rey, CA., Kent Estep of Santa Monica, CA., Austin Bordeau, of Brentwood, CA., Rick Austin of Pasadena, CA., John Krinski, of New York, Joe and Alice Rudnick of Brentwood, CA.

Leonard Fink, Attorney at Law, of Washington DC., Secretary and Director of the International Wildlife Conservation Society, for his many years of dedicated service to the society. Ronald Rosner, Esq., of New York, for his contributions in the area of zoological and historical records; Hikmat and Santa Bisht, of Mahendranagar, for their support and interest; Rajan and Sangita Bandhari of Katmandu, for much hospitality; Hem Bharal, Ph.D., of Katmandu, for his expertise as an ornithologist and his excellent WGP bird list contribution; Mr. Diwaker Chapagain, of Katmandu, Attorney at Law, Legal Adviser of the Department of National Parks and Wildlife Conservation and the World Wildlife Fund, for much assistance; Mr. Umesh Bista, of Mahendranagar, Attorney at Law and Project Manager of the new WGP Safari Lodge and Research Center, for dedicated service; Mr. Mangal Singh, of Mahendranagar, Project Engineer of construction of the new center, for his skills and dedication to the lodge construction project; Mr. Lok Thagarati, of Mahendranagar, Building Contractor of the new center, for his professional expertise; and Jangbu Sherpa, of Katmandu, my worthy Chef and Camp Manager of more than two decades, for devoted service.

Robert Rines and Joanne Hayes Rines, of Boston, MA., for their most generous support and contributions to the establishment of the new White Grass Plains Safari Lodge, Conservation and Research Center.

Chris Kraska and Laurie Faucina of Twinsburg, Ohio, for their valiant work and great personal interest in support of the initial construction of the lodge and their ongoing and most praiseworthy efforts towards its success.

Sian Pritchard-Jones and Bob Gibbons of Katmandu, Nepal and Chichester, UK, for their excellent job of editing the original manuscript and their enthusiastic assistance with publication.

And, last but never least, Mr. Rama Tiwari, Publisher and owner of Pilgrims Publishing of Katmandu, Nepal, and Varanasi, India, for his admirable fortitude in taking on the work.

ABOUT THE AUTHOR

One of the leading wildlife conservationists of Nepal, Peter Byrne spends up to eight months of each year in the field in that country. He is the author of a number of fascinating books linked to wildlife, including GENTLEMAN HUNTER, a study of man-eating tigers and leopards; TULA HATTI, THE LAST GREAT ELEPHANT, the story of his discovery of and association with the largest Asian elephant of all time; THE GREEN EYE, an exciting and unusual novel set in the Indo-Nepal region; and his autobiographical work, GONE ARE THE DAYS.

Peter Byrne was born and raised in Ireland and spent four years of World War II with the British Royal Air Force in southeast Asia. When the war came to an end, he joined a British tea company in north Bengal. After five years as a tea planter, he relocated to Nepal, where he opened up a professional big game hunting company. With some two decades of running safaris in Nepal's Terai forests behind him, he switched to wildlife conservation and he has now been engaged in this, in Nepal, for more than thirty years. He is currently (2007) building a safari lodge and research center in far west Nepal, at the edge of the White Grass Plains (WGP) Wildlife Reserve. His more than fifty years of fieldwork in the WGP are the background to this much-needed field guide to the park.

THE SOUTH WEST CORNER OF NEPAL, showing the general area of the Royal Sukila Phanta Wildlife Reserve. The western and southern boundaries of the park are contained by the Indian border.